# CODDLE
## YOUR
# CAT

# CODDLE
## YOUR
# CAT

## HOW TO PAMPER YOUR KITTY IN STYLE – PRACTICAL PROJECTS TO PROVE YOU CARE

Photography by Jane Burton
Text by Eve Devereux

LORENZ BOOKS
NEW YORK • LONDON • SYDNEY • BATH

**Disclaimer**

This book is intended as a light-hearted guide to coddling your cat, and it will provide hours of rewarding time with your pet. However, it is not intended as a care manual and any use is at the reader's sole discretion and risk. If in any doubt about the health of your cat you should consult a qualified veterinary surgeon.

This edition published in 1996 by Lorenz Books
an imprint of Anness Publishing Limited
administrative office: 27 West 20th Street
New York, NY 10011

© 1996 Anness Publishing Limited

Lorenz Books are available for bulk purchase for sales promotion and for premium use. For details write or call the manager of special sales, LORENZ BOOKS, 27 West 20th Street, New York, NY 10011; (212) 807-6739.

Produced by Anness Publishing Limited
1 Boundary Row
London SE1 8HP

ISBN 1 85967 111 X

Publisher: Joanna Lorenz
Senior Editor: Clare Nicholson
Consultant: Trevor Turner B. Vet. Med. M.R.C.V.S.
Special Photography: Jane Burton
Designer: Peter Butler and Susannah Good
Illustrator: Jane Molineaux

Printed and bound in Hong Kong

# CONTENTS

Introduction 6

Cat Napping 8

On the Catwalk 20

Gourmet Catering 30

Glamor Puss 44

Sports, Games, and Puss-times 56

Your Cat and the Stars 66

Cat Perks 80

Cat's Tips 92

Templates 92
Basic Sewing Techniques 94
Basic Stitches 95

Index and Acknowledgements 96

# Introduction

This is a book for you and for the cat (or cats) you love. In it you will find hundreds of inspirations and ideas for ways to express your affection and devotion to the animal who occupies the central position in your life, and dozens of practical projects which will add to the quality of your cat's existence. Discover how to make exquisite sleeping places and furnishings that will inject style and elegance into your cat's life. Learn how to give your cat, through fashion accessories and grooming, the hint of glamor that is every cat's desire and right. Create unforgettable meals that will thrill your companion's taste buds: every cat is a gourmet at heart and tempting treats are a sure way to strengthen the bond between you. Find out the games you can play with your cat, learn how to massage those feline tensions away, and on the spiritual side, uncover her mystic essence as revealed through awareness of the stars and their portents.

# Cat Napping

Top cats deserve the best, and battered baskets just won't do. Here's how to create the cat castles and kitty carriers of their wildest dreams, whether it be Captain Kitt's cabin for a tom or an empire-style bed for a princess puss, along with the ultimate in interior trimmings, cushions, drapes and rugs – whether these are to lie in, scratch on or chew.

A life of luxury is what every cat desires above all. So indulge your cat's fantasies and create a home where she will feel happy to spend her day – cleaning or snoozing or watching the world go by.

Your cat will naturally want to spend a lot of time on your bed (whether or not you happen to be in it) if she feels that her own facilities are anything less than first class. So make sure the cat home you create is more luxurious and seductive than your own, so you both get a good night's sleep.

This empire-style boudoir bed is fit for the feline queen who rules your humble home. Draw the curtains when she needs a little peace and quiet.

No corner or container will be left unexplored when a little kitty is looking for somewhere to sleep.

# Sitting Kitty

Statistically, your cat's principal hobby and "activity" will be snoozing, whether this is the full dream-filled sleep or the proverbial catnap. The amount of time and effort dedicated to this pursuit should be reflected in the elegance and suitability of the napping space. Here are a few inspired ideas for customized cat comfort and exquisite ambience. Either start from scratch or adapt your kitty's present resting place.

*House your cats in style: like the rest of us they don't like to be restricted to snoozing in the bedroom alone.*

*Wicker is fine for a desirable residence, but as these two would testify, it needs to be carefully lined for comfort.*

*For a really special treat, provide a superb four-poster bed where your prince in exile can dream those regal dreams that come at the end of a hard day's ruling. The witty leopardskin motif is printed on fur-friendly synthetic material, of course.*

# Captain Kitt's Cabin

*From catamaran to fleet fe-liner, any puss would love to be decked out like this sailor tom. Paint an old fruit crate and add some rope to provide a scratching post on long voyages.*

You will need:

*old box, such as a fruit crate • latex paints: blue, red and white • paintbrushes • PVA glue • long piece of rope • masking tape • two toy wheels or old bottle tops • thin cardboard • soft pencil • craft knife • stencil brush*

**3** Paint the toy wheels or bottle tops red and white, and leave to dry. Then to make a stencil of an anchor, draw an anchor on a piece of thin cardboard. Carefully cut it out with a craft knife, making sure you achieve a clear outline.

**4** To decorate the box, paint red and white stripes along the front and glue on the wheels. Secure the stencil to the box with masking tape then apply white paint with a stencil brush – do not overload the brush with paint otherwise it may smudge. Remove the stencil and allow to dry.

**1** Paint the inside and outside of the box with blue latex and leave to dry. Apply a second coat, if necessary.

**2** Glue the rope around the box, securing it with masking tape until it dries.

*For extra tom cat comfort and style, pad the box with a calico cushion stenciled with anchors.*

# Transports of Delight

Travel broadens the mind but, while some cats adore being taken to new venues, others express extreme reluctance. Once there, of course, even the coolest of cats gains boundless pleasure from investigating the novel locale – to the extent that you may have trouble getting them home again. Every cat wants to travel in style, so don't settle for a standard carrier unit: find or make something in which your companion can journey in luxury and comfort.

*For carrying your cat in true style, hat boxes make excellent travel compartments – no sharp corners or jagged edges to disturb or inconvenience.*

*Picnic hampers can make ideal carry-baskets, but make sure you line the inside with some padded blanket or soft quilted fabric. The aromas of old smoked salmon sandwiches and chicken breasts make for the perfect environment.*

## Jungle Carrier

*If you want your cat to stand out in the urban jungle, paint your carrier to make it fit for a lion king.*

**1** Paint the basket white and allow to dry. With masking tape, mark out an hexagonal area on both sides of the carrier, then paint the rest of the basket blue. Allow to dry and apply a second coat, if necessary. Within the white areas paint lions' faces in yellow.

*The ideal mode of transport for cats with a sense of adventure.*

## You will need:

*cat carrier • latex paints: white, blue, yellow, red and black • paintbrushes • masking tape • varnish • varnishing brush*

**2** Then paint the rest of the hexagon red. This will be the mane.

**3** When the paint is dry, add the facial features – eyes, nose, ears and mouth. Finally, to protect the carrier from the outdoor elements, paint it with a coat of clear varnish.

# Leopard-look De Luxe Carrier

*Fit for the boulevards of Paris, this high-style chic carrier is customized with fake fur fabric.*

## You will need:

*flat-packed cardboard carrier • craft knife • pencil • paper for pattern • leopard-print fabric, enough to cover box • pins • needle and matching thread • double-sided tape • bias binding • band • gold buckle*

**1** Take the flattened carrier and cut a large rectangle at both ends of the carrier to create ventilation holes for the cat. (The existing holes will be covered by the material.) Then use the flattened carrier to make a paper pattern. You will need one pattern for both ends and one to cover the middle section. Draw the ventilation holes on your pattern. (See diagrams on page 92.)

**2** Pin the patterns to the material and cut them out. Pin, baste and sew the two pieces of material which cover the inside and outside of each end, and the center pieces. Cut a hole for the handle to slip through and the ventilation holes too.

**3** Before you cover the box, attach some strips of double-sided tape as shown, to secure the material. Turn the edges of material over and secure with double-sided tape. Assemble the box then fit the side pieces of material onto the carrier. Secure with double-sided tape.

**4** To prevent the handles from fraying, stick double-sided tape onto bias-binding and attach to each edge. Fit the middle section of fabric over the rest of the carrier, sticking down any loose edges. Finally, embellish with a colored band and a smart gold buckle.

*Wild to be borne! Exotic, despotic and stylishly hypnotic, this sophisticated carrier will be well-spotted wherever you take it. Every trip will proudly remind your cat of the nobility of its ancestry.*

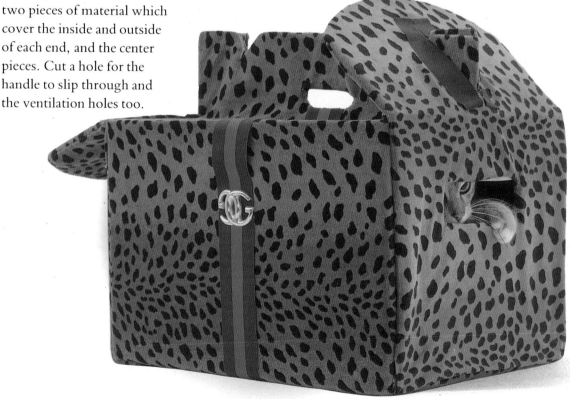

# Soft Furnishings

As everyone knows, cats are beings of infinite taste and discrimination – much more so, in most cases, than their owners. They take pride in their surroundings, and pleasure in their small luxuries. So, decorate your companion's space with meticulous attention to detail, try to furnish with flair and wit, and do keep your standards up to theirs.

*Just as dogs dream of rabbits, so cats dream of fish. And what better way to encourage such delicious dreams than a fish-embroidered mat . . .*

*Plaid brings out the best in cats, especially tabbies. The rich colors enhance the glowing warmth of the coat (and the pattern hides any loose fur).*

*For country cats, sometimes a simple cushion in unassuming folk style suits best.*

*Sweet thoughts are ensured with this temptingly-embroidered blanket.*

*Compliment your cat with a personal portrait. The texture of tapestry can encourage a little creative work of their own, so protect the work from playful scratches with plastic mounting.*

# Pawprint Cushion

*For festival days and special occasions, offer imperial-style comfort to your companion with this soft, luxurious velvet cushion. The stenciled pawprint pattern is specially designed to hide any muddy paw marks.*

**You will need:**

*tracing paper • soft pencil • thin cardboard • craft knife • ½yd upholstery velvet • scissors • stencil brush • black fabric paint • pins • needle and matching thread • 2yd multi-colored cord • four tassels • 16in cushion pad*

**3** Cut a 17in square from the velvet and place on a flat surface. Stencil pawprints at random, to look as if a cat has walked over the cushion. Hold the brush upright, and hold the stencil firmly in place to avoid smudging. Let dry.

**4** Make an envelope-style opening by cutting two 17 × 10in pieces of velvet. Place each piece over the stenciled velvet, right sides together, so that they overlap in the middle. Turn over and finish off the edges that overlap. Pin and baste, then sew around the outside, leaving a ¼in seam allowance. Turn right side out, trim with the cord and a tassel at each corner using stab stitch. Insert the cushion.

**2** Cut out the stencils with a craft knife.

**1** Trace the pawprint from the template on page 92. Transfer it onto the thin cardboard. Repeat the template once more, leaving a wide margin all around.

*The tassels provide a permanent toy on-site to help while away the hours.*

# Feline Furniture

Although accessories like the cat flap and the litter tray may not at first inspire creative flair, there is no need for them to be dull and drab. In fact it is precisely these functional items that require most thought and attention. The litter tray is a very important part of your cat's life: it can cause embarrassment but it needn't if you surround it with a lovingly crafted privacy screen. Show how much you appreciate your cat and respect her dignity by paying attention to her quality of life at all levels.

*A decorated doll's room becomes a perfect playpen for a little kitty.*

*Just to make sure no drafts disturb her, an exclusive insulator keeps your cat sitting pretty.*

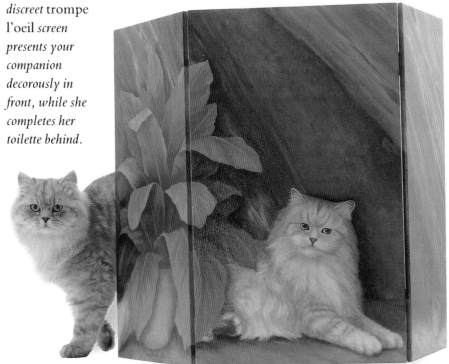

*A delightful and discreet* trompe l'oeil *screen presents your companion decorously in front, while she completes her toilette behind.*

*First impressions are vital, so don't let the entrance to your cat's environment be a boring plastic rectangle. With a little ingenuity you can make it an attractive and welcoming feature.*

# Skyscraper Privacy Screen

*This is the ideal way to hide your cat's litter tray from public view.*

## You will need:

*four rectangles of mat board: one 20 × 16in, one 21½ × 4in and two 18 × 10in • pencil • ruler • craft knife • four rectangles of masonite (dimensions as above) • paintbrushes • acrylic paints: black, terracotta, yellow and dark green • sponge • wood glue • upholstery tacks • four 1in hinges*

**2** Take the mat board and place it on top of its corresponding piece of masonite. Use it like a stencil to trace out the windows.

**3** Decide which windows you want to look dark and paint them black, and paint the door area terracotta. Then paint the rest of the masonite yellow

**4** Sponge the terracotta paint onto the mat board. Dilute the paint a little but not too much because if too wet it will warp the board. Decorate the three other pieces of masonite using the same technique and painting the front panel green and the sides terracotta.

*New York, New York! Both you and your companion will be grateful for your consideration in making this cosmopolitan privacy screen.*

**1** Decorate each piece of mat board in turn, starting with the tallest panel. Lightly draw the windows, door and cat's head onto the card. Cut them out with a craft knife.

**5** Glue all the pieces of mat board onto their corresponding pieces of masonite. Glue the skyscraper onto the central panel. Add on any additional features. Then, decorate the top edges with upholstery tacks and paint the back dark green. Join the two sides to the central panel with hinges.

# Finishing Touches

Your cat – and cats in general – are a very important part of your life, and you will want to embellish your home with images of your personal friend and other famous felines. You won't, of course, forget your cat's own interests while you go about this: make sure that some of your ornaments and hangings reflect your companion's passions – like a fun fish mirror before which she can clean and pose. With a little ingenuity there is hardly a decoration in your home that can't be "pussonalized".

*These lovely wooden ornaments could easily become toys if you don't keep a watchful eye.*

*Enhance a favorite feline photograph with a beautiful custom-made cat frame.*

*Birds on a line provide hours of amusement.*

*Wall decorations and plaques in cat-friendly motifs enhance any interior: the most popular designs in every catalog are mice, fish . . . and cats.*

# Fish Reflections

*Cats love gazing at their own reflection. So provide your companion with a deep-sea mirror.*

**You will need:**

*circular mirror • mat board • pencil • craft knife • scissors • corrugated cardboard • PVA glue • masking tape • modeling clay • strips of newspaper • wallpaper paste • acrylic paints: light green, pale blue, red and black • paintbrushes • glass beads • double-sided tape*

*Contemplating their reflection is as much a source of fascination for cats as it is for us.*

**1** Draw around the mirror onto the mat board. Draw a larger circle around this and use it as a guide to draw a basic fish shape. Cut out the outline – this will be the base – then a similar shape out of corrugated cardboard and glue it to the base. Cut several fins and scales from corrugated cardboard and build up a relief pattern.

**2** Cut a ½in wide strip of board long enough to fit around the outside of the mirror. Glue this around the mirror and stick the strip down bit by bit using masking tape. Around this carefully place a strip of modeling clay.

**3** Soak strips of newspaper in diluted wallpaper paste then start covering the corrugated cardboard. After the first layer is applied allow it to dry and then repeat the process several times.

**4** Paint the fish with acrylic paints, highlighting the features and scales with fine black lines. Stick on glass beads to create the effect of water bubbles. Finally, place strong double-sided tape on the back of the mirror and stick in place.

# On the Catwalk

Cats – males as much as females – are as "appearance-conscious" (ok, let's admit it, vain) as humans. Whereas most dogs are perfectly content to come home covered in mud and flop down to sleep, a cat wouldn't dream of being so sloppy. Your cat may spend hours each day ensuring perfect presentability, as every puss

wants to look her best at all hours of the day and night. Here are easy-to-sew projects for tailor-made, classic plaid winter coats or evening catsuits to kill for; along with daring accessories and high-style items such as the ultimate diamanté collar, the most stylish leash of the season, and a winter scarf. Assess the accessories and acquire the accoutrements – coats, collars, leashes and other vital items – that will set free the catwalk model trapped in the heart of every fashionable feline.

*Waiting on the podium to receive the gold medal for stylishness? Then wear this striking bright red halter encrusted with bold, daytime costume jewelry. This model presents paste with panache – and with a look that tells you in no uncertain terms that her real gems are locked in the safe back at the hotel!*

*Though more often associated with the dog world, leather and studs can be appropriated by the most delicate of felines to inject a hint of danger and machismo.*

# Overcats

Daytime strolls, a trip out in the car, a night out on the roof tops – your cat leads a rich life and will require a proper variety of suitable attire. Outside, cat coats keep your cat warm in winter and cool in summer. Inside, they are just unashamedly fun, frivolous indulgences to flaunt and enjoy.

*When there's a nip in the air, a light and airy jacket like this stenciled creation is just the ticket.*

*Sometimes, for those trips to town, a more sophisticated number is called for.*

# Plaid Kitty Coat

*The basic pattern for this coat can be adapted to suit every need. Add fur trimmings for evening outfits or use waterproof material for outdoors.*

You will need:

*plain paper for the pattern • pencil • scissors • 1yd × 45in plaid fabric • 1yd × 45in batting • 1yd × 45in lining fabric • safety pins • pins • needle and matching thread • bias binding • velcro hook and loop fasteners • hook and eye*

1 Scale up the template on page 93. Cut a square of the plaid large enough to take the pattern, then cut the batting and the lining larger. Place the batting on top of the lining then the plaid, and safety pin all the layers together.

2 With the safety pins holding the three layers firmly, machine- or hand-quilt a rectangular pattern across the surface. Then remove the safety pins.

3 Lay the paper pattern on top of the quilted fabric, then pin and baste it in position. Carefully cut around the pattern.

4 If you want the coat to fit snugly, sew a small dart in the center of the tail end of the pattern. Then remove the pattern.

5 Pin and sew the bias binding around the edge of the coat using slip stitch.

6 Sew velcro fasteners onto the flaps which will go under the chest.

7 To finish off, sew a hook and eye onto the neck opening of the coat.

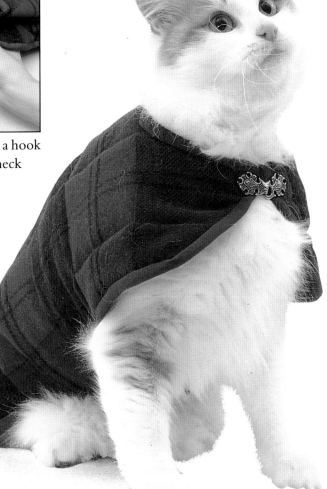

*The fuller cut on this outdoor cape is designed to protect during the severest winter. The perfect puss-suit for all pursuits.*

# Fancy Kit

When something more flamboyant is required, think Pussy Galore. There's no need to inhibit your imagination or your flair when assembling accessories for a suave, deliciously decadent affair. Shoot the works if your cat has a bit of Cat Woman or Top Cat inside (and what cat doesn't sometimes?), with a figure-hugging bodice or macho T-shirt.

*If it's smart enough for your cat it will be smart enough for you, too – just make sure that you also have the grace and poise to carry it off. When you go to the effort of giving your companion the coat of her dreams, keep going and make a stylish match for yourself.*

*A feather boa can be lots of fun – and who knows, she might even end up wearing it!*

For understated style and elegance, there's nothing to match the feel of pearls around her neck.

Leashing your cat is a tricky issue – it impacts on dignity and can cause hurt pride. So, where your companion is headstrong and safety demands caution, soften the blow by providing a beautifully crafted harness that can be worn with panache.

Of course, even the most aristocratic of cats occasionally wants to be a cool dude for a day. A trendy T-shirt is the ultimate in street style.

The last word in chic: this understated knit with its appliqué of gems is just the thing for the purebred cat. The pearls are imitation but the style is for real.

# Enchanted Circles

Getting the main costume right is only a beginning: complementary detail is everything. Of course, if your cat decides to wear nothing more than its fur, then there's nothing but the detail to work with.

The first detail you *have* to get right is the collar. Consider personality, bearing, coloring, appearance, physical style and presence, before you develop your designs. Obviously your cat needs a wardrobe full of collars for every occasion – these are just a few ideas.

*The perfect floral accessory for a picnic, christening, flower show, or any summer outdoor gathering. Why not embellish a straw hat for yourself with matching flowers?*

**3** Fold the picot-edged ribbon in half, and with matching cotton slip stitch the underside down to cover the raw ends of the ribbon on the back. Sew the buckle catch onto one end of the ribbon.

## Catmaiden Collar

*For a summer wedding, nothing is prettier than a floral decoration.*

### You will need:

*silk flowers in three different colors • 12 × ½in purple picot-edged ribbon • needle and matching thread • small glass beads • 8 × ¼in satin ribbon in gold and in green • ½in gilt buckle and catch • 3in small piece of elastic • bell*

**1** Remove the individual flowers from the main stalk and take out the plastic stamens. Starting 2in from one end, sew them firmly onto the picot-edged ribbon, alternating the colors. Stitch a bead into the center of each flower. Cover about 6in of the ribbon in this way.

**2** Cut 2in lengths from the gold and green satin ribbons and sew them onto the back of the picot-edged ribbon at intervals, twisting them into loops. Fold the stamens in half and stitch onto the ribbon in groups of two or three to fill any gaps.

**4** Attach the buckle to the elastic. Trim the loose ends of ribbon to length, so that the collar will fit the cat comfortably, then turn the raw edges under. Stab stitch the elastic between them, stitching firmly. Finish off by attaching a bell.

# Jeweled Collar

*Flair is simple to add: take a basic collar and embellish with jewels to transform it for a special occasion.*

**You will need:**

*double-sided tape • 8 × 2in black velvet ribbon • sew-on jewels in pinks and purples • needle and matching thread • small gilt buckle • 6 × 1in red velvet ribbon*

**1** Remove the backing from one side of the double-sided tape and stick it along the center of the wrong side of the black ribbon. Peel off the second backing paper and fold one of the long sides of the ribbon over the length of the tape.

**2** Sew on the jewels firmly along the folded edge, using a double length of thread, and arranging the colors alternately to form an interesting pattern. .

**3** Neaten the raw edges, then make a small loop at one end to enclose the buckle. Stitch in place. Make a fastening tab from the folded red ribbon at the other end.

*Ready for romance or romping: an all-purpose fun collar ideal for anything from a candlelit supper with someone special (maybe even you!) to a night on the town with the girls.*

**4** To finish off, fold over the loose side of the black velvet and stitch in place.

*This junior collar handcrafted in cheerful buttons is the ideal first fashion statement for the young at heart.*

# Vital Accessories

High fashion – especially for cats – is above all a joyously irreverant celebration of the unnecessary – which is why it is so enormously satisfying.

Slippers may have some small function for slouching around the house, or chewing on, but of course they should also look cool and sophisticated should visitors chance to call. Ribbons and bow ties are a frivolous delight, and you can expect a lot of hilarity as you attempt to tie them on. An elegant bow tie transforms any toe-tied tabby into Fred Astaire, while the touch of decadence created by a ribbon turns the shyest kitten into his Ginger Rogers.

*Thought for paws . . . these are the last word in affectation, and if Puss in Boots can't get used to lounging in them, she'll have enormous fun chasing them!*

*The simplest, and in many ways most elegant, accessory is a sleek satin ribbon.*

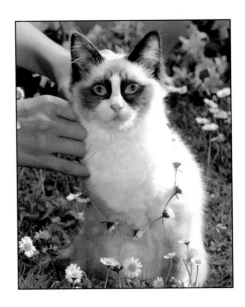

*A daisy-chain collar won't last longer than an afternoon, but will be a source of pride for both of you.*

*A comfortable scarf, casually worn, will impress friends and unexpected callers.*

# Bow Tie

*Any suave cat will need a range of these simple-to-make bow ties in different colors: from stylish black for formal wear, to bold tones and patterns for first nights, parties and celebrations.*

### You will need:

*12 × 12in white cotton fabric • embroidery hoop • soft pencil • gold outliner pen • fabric pens in a variety of colors • scissors • 8 × 8in red cotton fabric • pins • needle and matching thread • velcro • cat collar*

**1** Fasten the white fabric into the hoop. Support the fabric from behind then, using a soft pencil, mark out a rectangle 5½ × 3in for the bow and another 4 × 1½in for the central band. Leave room for seam allowances between the rectangles. Draw patterns on both rectangles then paint over with the gold outliner pen.

**2** Using the fabric pens, fill in the shapes. Color in the rectangles and a ½in seam allowance all around. Cut out the rectangles, including the seam allowance. Then cut two rectangles from the red fabric to the same size.

**3** Fold the edges under ½in to the wrong sides on both the painted rectangles and the red ones. Place the two rectangles for the bow together, wrong sides facing, and pin. Baste then sew them together. Repeat for the central band.

**4** Sew two rows of gathering threads along the center of the bow. Gather to make it approximately 1in deep. Machine- or hand-sew the central band to the front of the gathered bow tie.

**5** Finally, sew strips of velcro to the central band at either end. To finish fasten to a cat's collar.

*This sophisticated beau will dance tonight away with you in London, and buy you breakfast in Paris tomorrow morning.*

# Gourmet Catering

The way to every pet's heart is through its stomach. Kitty's senses of taste and scent are far more developed than our own, so it seems quite unfair to bore her with mass-produced fare. Start hunting for catnip and fish oil, and stock up on anchovies and sardines . . . these delectable recipes guarantee happier, healthier pets. From feline fish fancies to mackerel TV munchies, these are the flavors your four-legged friend will favor.

Although the easiest way to insure your cat enjoys a balanced diet is to feed her daily on canned cat food thoroughly mixed with a handful of fiber, once or twice a week serve up some kitty *haute cuisine* to add interest to the diet. Your cat will love the taste and texture of "real" food and appreciate the change: and you will enjoy giving her a tasty treat.

This stunning centerpiece is also the guest of honor! Like the rest of us, cats can sense, and love, a sophisticated setting, and any meal can be made an event with special touches such as these.

The treats in this chapter will certainly tip the scales. By all means pamper your pet with these gourmet delights and special delicacies – but do watch your companion's weight, as over-eating or any tendency to fat can be very unhealthy.

# TV Snacks and Titbits

When you're curled up in an armchair with your favorite snack and your fantasy movie star, don't forget your real loved one! Put together a selection of these feline foodstuffs and your cat will be right there snuggled up with you. Unless otherwise indicated, all recipes make one serving for one adult cat.

*Model goldfish might not taste very good, if they can be eaten at all, but Kitty will consider them an ideal hors d'oeuvre while you're in the kitchen agonizing between the caviar and the smoked salmon.*

# Eggstacy

*1 tbsp olive oil*
*1 egg*
*2 tbsp milk*
*¼ cup grated cheese*

Put the oil in a small frying pan and place over a low heat. Beat the egg and milk together. Once the oil looks medium-hot, slowly pour in the mixture, then gently agitate with a wooden spoon, ensuring the mixture doesn't start to fry. Add the grated cheese to the center of the mixture, and fold over the edges when firm. Cook until quite hard, cool, then cut into bite-sized pieces.

*The perfect brunch for those lying-in days*

*Sardine Soup is a fishy favorite*

# Sardine Soup

*2 canned sardines*
*pat of butter*
*1 cup water*
*few stalks of watercress*
*fish sauce (optional)*

Put the sardines and the pat of butter into a heavy-based frying-pan and place on a medium heat. As the pan warms and the butter melts, mash the sardines into it. When the butter has completely melted, pour in the water and stir as it comes to a boil. Thoroughly shred the watercress and toss into the pan. Remove the pan from the heat and allow to cool. Purée, and add a dash of fish sauce.

## Mouseburger Bites

*3oz sausage meat or finely
ground beef
2 tbsp oatmeal
1 egg, to bind
whisker of catnip, finely chopped*

Knead the ingredients together very thoroughly and form into a flat oval. Broil under a medium heat for 5–7 minutes, turning frequently, until the outside is crisp. Wait until cool, then slice into bite-sized chunks.

*Cheese delights for cat dreams*

*Sneaking downstairs for a midnight feast is not only the prerogative of small children . . .*

*Burger bliss for TV snacks*

## Cheese *Please!*

*½ cup grated cheese
2 tbsp plain yogurt or sour cream
a little oatmeal
2 tbsp margarine or low-fat spread*

Mash all the ingredients together, adding them in the order indicated above, and serve cold. No cooking is required for this dish. Some cats will not take to this dish as it is not meat-based: others will love it.

*CAT'S TIP*
*For a really quick gourmet treat, buy your cat a small package of luxury cat food and dice it up while it is still in its container – this is much more interesting than if you put it on a plate or in a bowl.*

*just a quick nibble, nothing more . . .*

*in fact no one's looking . . . total immersion.*

# Fish Fantasies

It is extremely rare to find a cat that doesn't adore seafood, yet often, having spent a lifetime eating the canned variety, they will be confused if you put raw fish in their bowl. Cooked fish is another matter and you will see their excited reaction when you start to prepare it. These fishy treats are certain to delight your companion.

# Nutrition

So far as useful nutritional content per ounce is concerned, fresh salmon is excellent, but fresh or canned sardines come close behind and are preferred by many if not most cats. Canned kippers, tuna or smoked mackerel are other good options.

If serving canned fish of any kind, it is a good idea to mash in some fiber in the form of oatmeal or cooked barley. With all fish dishes, make sure there is plenty of drinking water available in a separate bowl.

*Tasty trout treats*

# Crispy Trout Pieces

*Serves Two*

*1 egg yolk*
*1 small trout fillet*
*3 tbsp oatmeal*
*1 tbsp vegetable oil*

Preheat the oven to 350°F. Beat the egg, dip the fish in it, and then coat it with oatmeal. Put the oil in a small baking pan and lay the fillet in it, turning it over once or twice. Bake for 15 minutes, turn over, and bake for 15 minutes more. Remove the fish to a dish, allow to cool, and cut into bite-sized pieces.

Serving suggestion: if it looks a little dry, add a dash of cream.

*When it comes to finishing a tasty meal, a truly satisfied puss will sit and wash its face with its paw.*

*Canned pilchards*

*Heads and tails*

*Sliced kipper in cream*

## Mackerel Magic

*Serves Two*

*2 slices of unsmoked bacon, broiled*
*1 cup cooked brown rice*
*2 tsp soy sauce, Worcestershire or*
*fish sauce*
*1 fresh mackerel, headed, tailed, cleaned*
*and scaled*

Chop the bacon up small and mix with the rice, adding the sauce in dashes as you go. Broil the mackerel on both sides until crispy brown. Allow to cool, then split it along the stomach and gently open it out. Bone, working from head to tail. Fill with the rice and bacon mixture, close over the sides of the mackerel, and serve.

*Fish heaven for good cats*

*A fish in a dish*

## Kipper Suprême

*Serves Two*

*4oz cooked kipper*
*1 cup leftover cooked root vegetables*
*2 eggs*
*a little milk*
*½ cup grated cheese*

Preheat the oven to 325°F. Mash together the fish and vegetables. Put the mixture into an oiled baking pan. Beat the eggs, milk and cheese together, and pour on top of the fish mixture. Bake for about 20 minutes, until the outside is firm but the inside is reasonably soft. Remove from the oven and allow to cool.

*CAT'S TIP*
*Cats love plain smoked fish, but it is very salty and too much is not good for them. Whenever you eat it let your cat have just the skins and tails.*

## Kedgeree

*⅓ cup white rice*
*1 tomato, chopped*
*1 tbsp margarine or low-fat spread*
*3oz canned tuna or smoked mackerel,*
*skinned and boned*
*½ hard-boiled egg, shelled and*
*finely chopped*
*yolk of 1 egg*
*½ tbsp pouring cream*

Cook and drain the rice. While the rice is cooking, gently fry the chopped tomato in the margarine until soft. Add the fish and the egg and continue cooking, stirring all the time with a wooden spoon. Mix in the rice, still over the heat, and stir until everything seems steamy hot. Blend in the egg yolk, then the cream. After a last few stirs, tip onto a plate and allow to cool.

*Catty Kedgeree*

# Chicken Choices and Meat Treats

In general, poultry dishes are less calorific than meat recipes: gram for gram and ounce for ounce, skinned breast of roast chicken has little more than half the calories of a lightly fried hamburger. So, if your cat has a tendency to put on weight (not that you would ever comment, of course), serve poultry in preference – and try also to include vegetables and fiber in the form of bran, which have low calorific value and offer useful minerals. Always check cooked poultry very carefully for bones – these can be dangerous.

*Lean, keen and ready to preen. As all this lip-smacking confirms, plenty of chicken is essential in the diet of any health-conscious cat. It's an ingredient which they can comfortably fill up on without filling out.*

# Chicken Cheeseburger

*Serves Two*

*2oz finely ground beef*
*2oz finely ground chicken*
*1 tbsp canned thick chicken soup*
*2oz whole grain bread crumbs*
*or oatmeal*
*1 baby carrot, cooked until soft*
*1 egg*
*½ cup grated cheese*

Mash the meat and chicken with the soup, then add the bread crumbs or oatmeal, mushy carrot and egg. Make into two small burgers and broil (leaving much rarer than you would for yourself). Sprinkle with grated cheese and broil again until the cheese is melted. Allow to cool until warm to the touch, and serve. (Why not broil one of the burgers for longer and eat it yourself? That way you can genuinely share a meal with your companion.)

*Mince magic for cats*

*Surf "n" turf, cat-style*

## Chicken with a Sardine Crust

*Serves Two*

*1 can sardines in olive oil*
*1/4 cup whole grain bread crumbs*
*1 egg, beaten*
*1/2 tsp brewer's yeast*
*2 cooked chicken drumsticks,*
*bones removed*

Drain the sardines, reserving the olive oil, and mash. Mix in the bread crumbs, egg and yeast to an even, gooey consistency. Coat the chicken drumsticks evenly in the mixture. Heat the reserved olive oil in a frying pan, then add the coated drumsticks and fry, turning frequently, until brown. Remove from the heat, and cool before serving.

## Rabbit Chasseur

*Serves Two*

*3–4 canned prunes, pitted*
*1 tbsp vegetable or olive oil*
*3oz rabbit, cut into*
*1/4in cubes*
*1 tbsp flour*
*1 tbsp tomato juice*
*1–2 pinches of chopped catnip*
*1 tbsp canned thick chicken soup*

Mash the prunes coarsely on a plate, then heat the oil in a frying pan and add the diced pieces of rabbit, frying them until they are pale brown. Add the mashed prunes, stir and sprinkle in the flour and stir. Continue frying until the coated pieces are a golden brown. Remove the pan from the heat and immediately add the tomato juice, catnip and soup, continuing to stir gently for a further 2–3 minutes. Remove the food from the pan to a separate dish and allow to cool before serving.

*Run rabbit, run rabbit . . .*

*Truly meaty morsels*

## Organ Duet

*1 chicken liver, finely chopped*
*1/2 lamb's kidney, finely chopped*
*2 strips of bacon,*
*finely chopped*
*1 baby carrot, cooked*
*1 tbsp whole grain bread crumbs*
*or oatmeal*

Put the meat into boiling water for 3 minutes. Drain off the water, then blend the meat with the carrot and bread crumbs or oatmeal for a few seconds (leave some texture), or mash the mixture together with a fork. Cool until warm to the touch. Serve up with a sprig of parsley.

*CAT'S TIP*
*To add an extra treat, serve a dish of catnip tea. Simply pour boiling water onto shredded catnip leaves (3–4 tsp catnip per 1 pint). Once cool, cover, and keep in the fridge.*

# Entertaining with Ease

Always feed your cat before inviting her friends round: unless she is unusually well-adjusted, she is likely to resent the intrusion of other cats onto her "turf", no matter how friendly she might be under different circumstances. Feeding in advance will lower the tension and put everyone at their ease. Then it is a good idea to keep back a little treat for her – something as simple as a bowl of milk – as a symbol of her proprietary rights. The guests should be served on "neutral" plates – not your companion's regular bowls and dishes.

## "EtiKit"

Give each cat a separate dish, and serve everyone at once, or at least in quick succession. Once a cat is comfortable with its own plate, squabbles are unlikely so long as the portions are equal and everyone has enough to eat.

If the cats are old friends and are used to eating together, you can risk serving the banquet for the entire company in a single dish. There will inevitably be some jostling, but usually it will be fairly good-natured.

*Entertaining can be a nerve-racking experience for kittens, so let them get used to it gradually and make allowances for lapses in table manners.*

*It is never too early to teach the basics of floor etiquette. These two kittens have learned the art of politely taking turns, and thus will enjoy social gatherings much more.*

*Party time for fruity cats*

## Fruit Cocktail

*2 tsp melon, cut up fine*
*2 tsp white grapes (seedless), cut up fine*
*2 tsp kiwi fruit, cut up fine*
*1 segment tangerine, cut up fine*
*1–2 tbsp cream*

Mix up the fruit together, pour on the cream and fold in. Serve chilled.

## Salmon Mousse

*4oz cooked salmon, skin and
bones removed
½ cup skimmed milk
1 tbsp margarine, softened or
low-fat spread, creamed
1 drop red food coloring
several cooked, shelled shrimp
up to ½ cup prepared gelatin*

This party dish always impresses.
The quantities serve three or four as a
main course – or twice that many as a
starter.

Mash the cooked salmon and
gradually add the milk; alternatively,
put the cooked salmon and the milk
in a blender or food processor and
process until creamy. Stir in the
margarine or low-fat spread, add the
food coloring, and beat vigorously
until stiff. Put in a glass bowl or a
mold so that the mixture fills it by
three-quarters. Chill for 20 minutes,
then decorate with the cooked
shrimp, and pour on just enough
heated gelatin to cover them. Once
this layer has set, add further gelatin
to taste and leave for an hour or two
in a cool place or the fridge. To
serve, turn the mousse out onto a
plate and divide into portions.

*Sensational salmon*

*Fishy treats*

## Fabulous Fishballs

*Serves Eight*

*3 baby carrots, cooked until soft
8–16oz canned tuna in
olive oil, drained
2oz cooked herring, skin removed
2 tbsp whole grain bread crumbs
or oatmeal
2–3 tbsp grated cheese
2 tsp brewer's yeast
several pinches chopped catnip
1 egg, beaten
2 tbsp tomato paste (not ketchup)*

Preheat the oven to 350°F. Mash the
carrots with the fish, bread crumbs
or oatmeal, cheese, brewer's yeast,
catnip, egg and tomato paste to an
even paste. Mold into small balls and
put on a greased baking tray. Bake
for 15–20 minutes, checking
frequently: the fishballs should be
golden brown and feel firm. Cool
thoroughly.

# Special Occasions

It's important to bring your pet into family festivities like Christmas, birthdays, Easter and Halloween. You might find that (rather like humans) they will feign indifference at first, but more usually they will become tremendously excited and get into everything, making an awful nuisance of themselves.

## Birthday Suggestion: Celebrity Fishsticks

As a little extra to be offered on this most special occasion, take a commercial frozen fishstick and thaw it out. Mash it and shape it into your cat's favorite fantasy – a mouse, a fish, or even a significant other cat.

Commercial fishsticks have already been cooked, so you can serve this dish cold, or bake it for 10 minutes in a medium oven (350°F), then cool.

*Shaped to perfection*

# Valentine's Day

If you can bear to serve your companion a bad pun on Valentine's Day, do remember that cats *love* heart.

More in harmony with the spirit of the occasion would be heart-shaped morsels: most of the "burger" and baked recipes in this book can be molded in this way. Or pipe heart motifs on any favorite dish – use mashed potato on hot food or cream on cold.

*My heart belongs to you*

## All My Heart

*¼ green or red bell pepper, diced*
*½ tbsp olive oil*
*2oz beef heart, very finely diced*
*¼ cup grated cheese*

Fry the pepper for a couple of minutes in the olive oil. Add the heart and keep frying until it starts to brown. Put everything in a bowl and, while it is still hot, mash in the cheese. Cool and serve.

# Easter

Around Easter, you should be able to find egg molds. These make the perfect special occasion serving dish for Easter.

## Easter Scramble

*1 tsp butter, margarine or*
*low-fat spread*
*2 medium-sized eggs*
*½ cup skim milk*
*chopped catnip to taste*

In a small saucepan melt the butter or fat slowly over a very low heat. Beat the eggs, milk and catnip together, pour into the pan, and stir vigorously. Keep stirring, more gently, until the mixture scrambles, then remove from the pan, and cool. Tip the scramble into an egg mold and serve. (It's probably wise not to give your cat any further egg-based dishes for a few days.)

*Cat eggstravaganzas*

# Halloween

Buy a small rutabaga or turnip and hollow it out. Carve the front with eyes, nose and mouth, but not right through: leave a thin membrane of flesh between the internal hollow and the carved features. Put a candle or nightlight inside, light it and the features should glow spookily. Your cat will find this a fascinating object, but don't push her too close, and don't allow the candle to burn too long. When your cat gets bored with the toy, allow it to cool, remove the candle and pour in a tasty mixture that she will love to scoop out, such as cod fish roe.

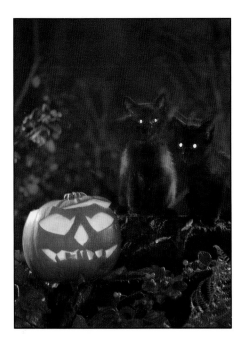

*The wild spirit within your cat comes into its own at Halloween . . .*

*Something fishy*

# Roe Dip

*1 tomato, peeled and
very finely chopped
1 tsp olive oil
4oz cod fish
1 generous tbsp pouring cream*

Fry the tomato in the oil until soft and translucent, then remove from the pan. Crumble the roe, and mash in the cream and then the tomato, either in a blender or by hand, until you have a smooth, creamy texture. Chill in the fridge, then scoop generously into the Halloween mask or turn into a mold for a birthday dish.

# Christmas and Thanksgiving

Naturally your cat will be an essential guest, so roast a small chicken (*poussin* in French) before you start roasting the turkey for the rest of the family. Let your cat savor the aroma of the bird while hot, but no picking at this stage, as the small bones can be dangerous. Cool the small chicken in the fridge while you're roasting the turkey; then bone it, carve the meat, and serve with seasonal garnishes.

*Puss poussin*

*CAT'S TIP*
*Note that while cats can cope with raw egg yolks, uncooked whites are extremely bad for them, as they contain an enzyme that breaks down biotin, a vitamin your cat needs: never serve your cat raw egg white in any shape or form.*

# Designer Dishes and Customized Catlery

Dishes decorated in appropriate motifs can bring a little extra magic to supper time – as can cat mats and all the other accessories and atmospheric additions that enhance the perfect dining environment.

*If you decorate your dishes with cats such as these then carry the theme through to the rest of the table accessories.*

*Putting the finishing touches to the table setting before the guests arrive.*

# Mice and Cheese Plates

*If you are lucky, you may come across china that is already decorated with your cat's favorite motifs. Otherwise, it is easy to make your own designs – painted freehand, stenciled or stamped. Use paints that are non toxic, as the dishes may come in for a good licking.*

*It doesn't take long – or require any previous artistic training or great skill – to paint the bowls and plates you use for your cat's meals.*

## You will need:

*plain white ceramic plate • black, non toxic, water-based craft enamel (for use on ceramics) • fine paintbrush*

1 Clean and dry the plate thoroughly. Using the black enamel, paint the mice around the edge of the plate. When dry, paint the mouse in the center, making long, thin, tapering strokes for the whiskers. Place the plate into a cold oven and bake for 30–45 minutes at 325°F. Do not remove until it has cooled.

# Pussy Place Mat

*This simple place mat will help keep the floor around kitty's food bowl nice and clean. Make sure that the central fish motif is slightly larger than your cat's bowl so that the head and tail poke out from under the bowl.*

You will need:

*colored felts • scissors • fabric glue • clear plastic • paintbrush • needle and thread*

**1** Cut out the basic shapes from felt. You will need a larger square; two oval shapes, one slightly larger than the other; a smaller oval shape; a fish shape; several small white circles; and four small stars.

**2** Assemble the design as shown in the picture, then carefully glue the pieces in place.

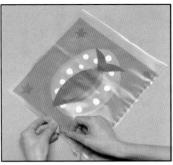

**3** To protect the mat, trap the felt between two pieces of clear plastic. Sew around the edge with running stitch. Cut away any excess plastic.

*Charming, simple and transforms a snack into a feast – a gift that will be appreciated and used time and again.*

# Glamor Puss

Every pusscat likes to look good on the roof tops, and time spent in the bathroom and boudoir is an essential part of the daily regime. This chapter provides invaluable advice on how to create the appropriate setting, with full techniques for perfect puss presentation and beauty care treatments.

All cats need to be pampered, and the ultimate wash-and-brush guide gives grooming techniques, massage and aromatherapy tips, home beauty-parlor treatments and decorative fur stylings.

Your cat is already beautiful to you – but she also needs to feel consistently good about herself. This is how to go about it.

Cleaning and grooming make for a
healthier, happier cat: inner contentment
and well-being will follow naturally
from external trimness, glossiness and
feline elegance.

A personal vanity case for special cat care
accessories is an essential part of the
wardrobe.

# Bathed in Splendor

This is not a question of hygiene: most cats are so scrupulous in their habits and personal cleanliness that they never actually need a bath at all. What is under discussion here is *pampering* – the indulging in the sybaritic pleasures of the bath. Although cats don't enjoy the sensation of luxuriating in scented waters like the rest of us, if you accompany the bathing with lots of stroking, petting and massaging, it will ensure complete cat heaven.

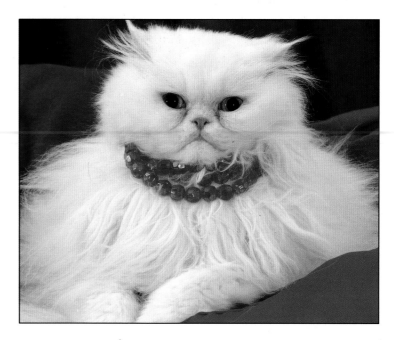

*Bathed, powdered and perfumed – all dressed up and ready to go.*

*Introduce your kittens to the concept of bathing and grooming at an early age.*

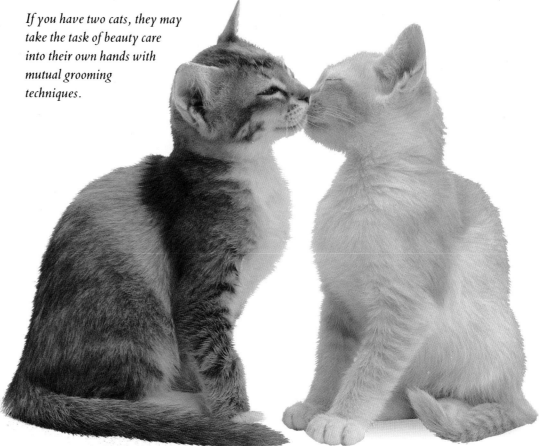

*If you have two cats, they may take the task of beauty care into their own hands with mutual grooming techniques.*

Bathtime Accessories
*A couple of cotton wool balls*
*A shower attachment*
*Cat shampoo (don't use regular human shampoos)*
*A good cat comb or brush*
*A portable hair-dryer*
*Soft, scented towels*

*Of course, with few exceptions, cats are instinctively clean: any cat will groom itself far better than you could hope to. Your cat's first step is to lick clean the paws; then to use tongue and paws to clean every inch of the body.*

# Bathtime

*For the ultimate bathtime experience, flickering candles and subdued music will set the mood.*

### You will need:

*washing bowl and pitcher • cat shampoo • natural sponge • several large towels • brush and comb*

**1** Fill a bowl half full with warm water. Test the temperature, then lift the cat into the bowl and hold firmly. Wash with warm water, making sure the fur is really wet, then apply the shampoo, following the manufacturer's instructions. Massage the shampoo into the cat's coat but do not get shampoo in her eyes.

**2** Rinse the cat with warm water, making sure that all the shampoo is out of her coat. Then take several large, warm, soft towels and gently rub dry.

**3** Finally, start a long and luxurious session of gentle combing, making sure that you get out all of the snarls. For speed you can use a hair-dryer but your cat may not approve.

# Good Grooming

Cats adore being groomed: the combination of stroking, attention and tidying makes them purr euphorically. When your companion gets the habit you will need to spend more and more time keeping her happy – not something that is likely to be a problem for you!

Start the grooming session with a period of preliminary caressing with the fingers. Stand your cat facing away from you and softly stroke all over her body, gently massaging the skin and feeling the fur for any dirt or matted areas. You will then be ready to proceed to the more advanced techniques described on these pages.

*A rubber brush is ideal for massaging your cat. Work with circular movements and she is sure to help you by manoeuvering as you go.*

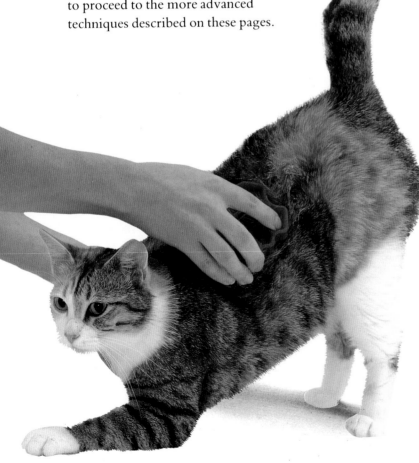

## Grooming a Short-haired Cat

*Short-haired cats need very little grooming as they are very adept at keeping themselves clean. However, they certainly won't say no to a little extra help, particularly if you incorporate a little massage into the routine.*

**1** Introduce your cat to the tools of the trade.

**2** Start by grooming with the metal comb, working down the sides.

### You will need:

*metal comb • rubber brush • coat conditioner • soft cloth*

**3** Continue combing from head to tail.

**4** Use the rubber brush to remove any loose hair, and apply a few drops of coat conditioner.

**5** Finish off by using the cloth to shine the coat.

# Grooming a Long-haired Cat

*Grooming has two objectives: a beautifully turned-out companion; and a relaxed, good-natured friend.*

**You will need:**

*wide-toothed comb • rubber brush*

**1** Start by combing out all the difficult knots and tangles in the coat.

**2** Work your way down the sides and then under the chest.

**3** Don't forget the tail. Make sure you gently comb out all of the knots.

**4** You may need to untangle some of the snarls with your hands.

**5** To get out some of the loose hair, comb your cat's fur upwards.

**6** Use a rubber brush to get out old fur. Work with circular movements.

**7** Soon your cat will be treating this as a game.

*Whether short-haired or long-haired, you need a mirror to admire the results.*

*All primed for first prize in the cat show . . . and ready to have another session with the comb.*

# Vanity Accessories

The number of different grooming and beauty tools a cat requires is not huge – but over time, as with any much-loved hobby, you will accumulate dozens of perfect little items, including a special gadget for each small task. Any good pet store will be able to supply you with the basics; after that, use your skills as a collector and artist to find and fashion your own customized range.

*Remember, grooming time should be fun for both of you, and will be even more appreciated if everything looks enchanting.*

# Fancy Brush

*Even the most dignified of long-haired cats can get into a tangle even through the most innocent romp. Making this decorative brush will persuade them to endure the indignity of tidying themselves up.*

**You will need:**

*small, soft-bristled wooden brush • sandpaper • gold acrylic paint • paintbrush • silver doilie • scissors • PVA glue • rhinestones in various colors • mat craft varnish • varnishing brush*

**1** Sand the brush to remove any varnish, smooth down the surface, then paint gold. Allow to dry and apply a second coat if necessary.

**2** To decorate the brush, select small, interesting motifs from the paper doilie and cut out neatly. Stick down with PVA glue.

**3** Embellish the brush by adding rhinestones and coat with a layer of mat varnish (avoiding the jewels) to protect the cut-outs.

# Vanity Case

*All of your cat's vanity accessories can go into this elegant case, to be brought out whenever it's time for a grooming session.*

### You will need:

*pink silk or satin lining • scissors • hat box • double-sided tape • thin cardboard • small amount of batting • glue • paintbrush • tiger-print fabric • handbag mirror • needle and matching thread • gold tassel • pencil • ½yd gold cord*

**1** Cut a strip of pink fabric to cover the inside and outside of the rim of the box lid, allowing an extra 1in on both the width and the length. Stick in place using double-sided tape and neaten the raw ends. From thin cardboard, cut a circle the same size as the lid. Stick on a circle of batting to give a padded effect, then cover with fur fabric.

**2** Glue the fur-covered circle to the top of the lid. Then cut a smaller disc out of cardboard to fit inside the lid and cover with lining fabric. Attach the mirror to the center with double-sided tape. Secure the disc inside the lid using double-sided tape.

*Perfect for home or travels abroad – try to choose a shade of fake fur that does not clash with your cat.*

**3** Sew the tassel onto the center top of the lid.

**5** Line the inside of the box with pink fabric. Cut a disc of cardboard slightly smaller than the base and cover it too. Glue in place so that it covers the raw edges of the lining in the box.

**4** Put the lid onto the box, then draw around the rim. Using this guideline as the top edge, cover the main box with fur fabric. Pierce a hole halfway down each side and thread the cord to form a carrying handle.

**6** Cut a strip of fabric slightly larger than the height of the box and 2in longer than its circumference. Fold it in half and sew the short ends together to form a circle. Neaten the two long edges, then stitch six equal compartments. Finally, attach to the box with double-sided tape.

# Aromatherapy

For centuries, the pure essences of aromatic plants have been valued for their luxurious scents and their many life-enhancing properties, and your pet will naturally enjoy indulging in the same kind of sybaritic "scentsual" experience as you do.

Appropriately, it is the Egyptians – worshippers of the noble cat – who get credit for recognizing the full physical and spiritual properties of aromatic essences, and who developed the art from ritual and ceremonial use to massage and personal pleasure.

Your cat will enjoy the beneficial effects of aromatherapy in many ways. Herbal tea bags, if not used for infusions as such, are often appreciated as scented toys in their own right. Fresh herbs, or their dried versions, can be brushed against, nibbled at, or played with. And of course your cat will no doubt appreciate, with you, the more subtle effects of aromatic candles and scents. A lingering fragrance can clear the air and promote pleasant thoughts for both cat and owner.

*Your cat will be intrigued and fascinated by the range of smells emanating from your aromatherapy kit. (Keep all bottles tightly sealed – essential oils must never be taken internally.)*

*A dog-shaped toy is tantalizingly stuffed with scented catnip – guaranteed to send your friend into a heightened state one way or the other.*

**Important Note:** Herbs and spices, used fresh, should not harm your cat at all. If you use them in essential oil form then remember that they are very powerful and use only in highly diluted form and follow the labels precisely; don't allow your cat to drink them, and don't use them around pregnant cats. Essential oils can be wonderful natural therapies and remedies, but are never a substitute for proper vetinary advice if your cat is ill – the list opposite is intended as a light-hearted guide.

**Basil** A herb for depression and the more nervous cat.

**Bay** A possible remedy for sleeplessness (not usually a cat-related problem, of course).

**Chamomile** An ideal sedative, again not always necessary with snooze-prone pets.

**Cinnamon** A useful pick-me-up and general tonic, for sluggish cats.

**Eucalyptus** Good as a head-clearer, perhaps after a heavy night on the back fence.

**Frankincense** Encourages a more meditative state, perhaps appropriate for the more fractious tomcat.

**Jasmine** A luxurious flower that will lift the spirits.

**Lavender** A pleasant tranquilizing scent that is popular with cats.

**Marjoram** Another herb that will calm and soothe.

**Myrrh** Usually used for indigestion, perhaps after a day of over-indulgence.

**Peppermint** A very popular herb with cats (used peppermint herbal tea bags provide hours of fun).

**Pine** Good, of course, for breathing difficulties and chills.

**Rosemary** A good pepping-up herb that will aid concentration.

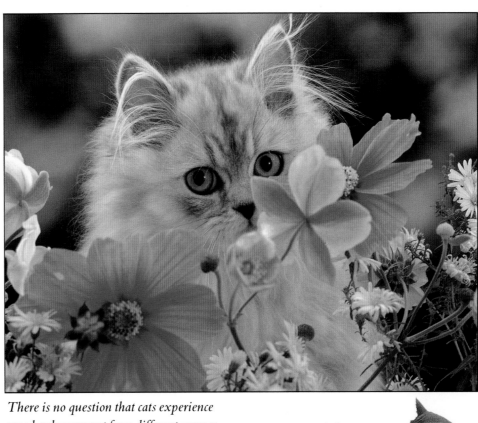

*There is no question that cats experience mood-enhancement from different aromas – their sense of smell is much more highly developed than that of humans.*

*The aromatic herb* par excellence *is of course the irresistible catnip plant.*

# Massage

Massage for cats and kittens is an extension of "finger grooming" – and this gentle all-over body rub is the best place to start any massage session. Once your efforts have built up a steady, appreciative purr – you'll be surprised how loud the noise can get – move on to gently caress the rest of your cat's body.

Every once in a while you might think of using some of your own perfumes to give your cat a special treat. *Be very careful though* as highly perfumed toiletries can irritate cats.

*A firm back stroke followed by a quick flick up to the tail is an irresistible massage technique that will delight every cat.*

*The cat prepared for massage . . . creating the right ambience is all-important, as for humans, so have soft towels and the right props at hand.*

# Massage Sequence

*Massage is enjoyed instinctively by cats – one always has the impression that they know a lot more about it than we do.*

**2** Now shift your attention to her chest, reaching round in front with both hands to press the center of the chest, moving the pressure outwards, then circling back to the center to start again.

**3** Next come the sides, which you can knead more firmly, using both your fingertips and the heels of your hands, running the pressure in a general direction from the neck towards the tail.

**4** A good kneading of the shoulders is often appreciated, and you can try running your thumbs gently down the length of your cat's spine, again from neck to tail. Most cats cannot abide having their tummies rubbed; but a few adore it, and will roll ecstatically over on their backs to make your task easier – rubbing with the front of the knuckles in a rotary motion is best.

**1** Caress your cat gently behind the ears, either both at the same time or one after the other.

*The final stage of a successful massage – complete relaxation from whiskers to tail tip.*

**6** . . . and back to the head, which may need a a slow rubbing with the knuckles.

**5** Failing this, your cat may enjoy it if, with her facing away from you, you massage her flanks with your fingertips . . .

# Sports, Games, and Puss-times

The sport cats enjoy most, of course, is sleeping, in all its myriad forms – dozing, resting, snoozing and stretching. A full guide to all the techniques involved in these important exercises is provided in this vital chapter. However, when they aren't pursuing the above, there are occasions when your cat will choose to exert

herself in more active pursuits, such as chasing, scratching, watching and catching things.

All cats remain kittens at heart, and love to play. And of course as well as giving pleasure, frequent games will have therapeutic effects for your pet, providing stimulation and exercise, and keeping them bright-eyed and sharp-clawed.

All work and no play makes for a dull companion. Every cat needs to be stretched both physically and intellectually to fulfil itself – and there is no better way than through toys, games and sports. For a complete cat, always provide lots of stimulation – good food and a warm bed are only half the job.

Toys of all sorts help cats acquire and enjoy new skills, and learn about the world and their role in it. Here, a playmate stuffed with catnip convinces this young cat that perhaps dogs aren't so bad after all!

# Snoozing

For cats, there is an art to snoozing, which we humans will never fully understand. The feline snooze *artiste* displays a range of positions and perfectly executed techniques which have evolved over the years – and even the least proficient of cats can far surpass anything a human has ever attempted.

Just a few of the basics are outlined below: your cat will demonstrate many personal variations on these principle "asanas" as well as countless thousands of other positions which we haven't space to examine here.

## Sprawled on Side, One Rear Leg Raised

Most commonly occurs when your cat realizes the time is right for an impromptu snooze midway through a bout of self-grooming. This advanced technique, combining a certain decadence with an undercurrent of humor, is dearly loved by connoisseurs.

# Shelf Posture, with Tail and One Foreleg Dangling

As the name suggests, this is best accomplished on a shelf containing highly fragile and irreplaceable ornaments, although many cats will also produce graceful extemporizations using the back of an expensively upholstered chair. Often the tail can be twitched to and fro to show that snoozing is not just a static artform but one more closely allied to ballet or t'ai chi.

## The Doormat

A room bathed in sunlight or the carpet in front of a roaring log fire is a suitable location for this whole-hearted posture. The skill is to make it look as if the body has been transformed into a flattened and lifeless bed of fur.

*Don't worry! Out of necessity their physiology has evolved over thousands of years to allow sleep to occur naturally in every conceivable contortion.*

**Going** . . . *To create the mood for snoozing, start by rubbing your finger seductively behind the ear . . .* **going** . . . *slide round behind the head and nuzzle gently with the palm . . .* **gone** . . . *and leave her dreaming contentedly.*

*A nice variation, with the right foreleg neatly tucked under the chin. This cat (above) scored triple ZZZ in the Nap Olympics, snoring away with a gold medal for technical merit and stylistic excellence.*

*In training, and dreaming of emulating the legendary slumbers of its ancestors, this cat (below) shows complete disregard for the rules of grace, style and form, but scores high on appeal.*

*In another category, Assisted Snooze, this moggie (right) cuddles up to her favorite scarf for cosy comfort.*

*Soma Vulgaris (above) – known in the trade as "self-nesting". This is the common or garden "Furball" style, which all cats will fall back on for everyday use.*

# Toys and Games

Toys can be improvized from all sorts of objects around the house, and you can have tremendous extended game sessions using something as simple as a spoon. However, probably because of the intensity with which they enjoy their play, cats can very soon tire of a particular toy, so you will need a constantly changing list of fabulous playthings on demand. The best idea if you want to keep your cat contented is to surround her with lots of entrancing toys, both simple and complicated, both incidental and specially made.

*All cats have predatory instincts. If no natural prey animals are in evidence, then hunting-toys like these stuffed mice are a wonderful and socially acceptable substitute. The colors don't matter: this one is in rainbow colors so you can spot it easily when it has rolled behind the back of the bookshelf.*

*You could make these mice even more tantalizing by making them into a mouse mobile.*

# Paper Mice

*Paper mice won't last for ever, but they're easy to make, decorative, and offer variety and novelty.*

## You will need:

*4in square of paper • craft knife • pencil*

**1** Crease the paper along its diagonal, then open the paper out again. Bring in the side to make a kite shape, creating a sharp corner at the bottom.

**2** Fold the kite shape in half. With a craft knife, cut a V-shaped slit to create the ears. Fold each "V" shape upwards.

**3** To create the tail, fold the paper forward, about half the way along, then fold it back on itself again. Draw in the eyes and curl the tail.

# Goldfish-bowl Ball

*Make sure you choose washable non-shrink, colorfast fabrics – test-wash first if you're unsure.*

### You will need:

*tracing paper • soft pencil • thin cardboard • scissors • 1/3yd of 1yd wide strong, blue fabric • 10 × 8in yellow fabric, backed with iron-on interfacing • 4 × 4in paler blue fabric • scrap of green fabric • pins • needle and matching thread • scraps of interfacing • strong button thread • four gold beads • four flat circular plastic squeakers • toy stuffing • piping cord • blue bias binding*

**1** Transfer the pattern on page 93 onto cardboard. Cut out the pattern pieces: six main pieces in blue, four fish shapes in yellow, a pale blue circle for the top of the bowl, and green leaves.

**2** Draw a stem onto one of the blue segments. Pin and baste the leaves into position along the stem. Pin a scrap of interfacing behind the blue fabric. Using a machine satin stitch, appliqué the leaf and stitch the wavy stem.

**3** Join the appliquéd segment to two other blue segments, and sew the other three blue segments to each other, along the stitching lines, making two half balls. Trim the seams. Don't join the two halves together at this stage.

*Your cat can while away hours with a simple toy – so imagine how much fun this ball with squeakers inside will provide.*

**5** Join the two halves of the ball together. Trim the seam. Join the top and bottom of the last seam, leaving a gap. Stuff the ball firmly with toy stuffing. Slip stitch the opening securely.

**6** Enclose the piping cord in the bias binding, and pin onto the pale blue fabric circle. Stitch into position. Turn the circle over, and, enclosing the raw edges, slip stitch it to the top of the ball.

**4** Using strong button thread, sew the fishes' eyes into position. Pin then baste two fish onto each half of the ball, enclosing a squeaker as you do so. Satin stitch around each fish.

# Rugged Pursuits

The outside world holds all kinds of delicious fascinations – whether it's a garden teeming with wildlife; a back alley; an open field or a fishpond. If your cat is confined in the city then you can easily bring the great outdoors indoors by making toys and games which are evocative of the world outside.

*The fact that someone put this entrancing object in the garden for birds, not kittens, is of no relevance whatsoever. They believe it has been erected solely to amuse them.*

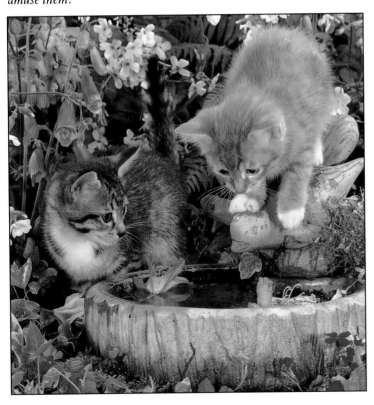

*To make these robins even more tasty, you can fill them with catnip instead of toy stuffing.*

# Felt Robins

*The purrfect way to introduce your cat to her favorite outdoor pursuit – chasing birds.*

**1** Trace the pattern pieces from the template on page 92 onto thin cardboard, then cut them out of felt. For each bird you will need two body pieces in red felt, two wings in green felt, one gusset in red felt, a beak in yellow felt and eyes in black felt.

**3** Sew the two body pieces together, along the top seam, right sides together. Then sew the gusset in place, leaving a gap for filling. Turn right side out.

## You will need:

*tracing paper • soft pencil • thin cardboard • scissors • felt: red, green, yellow and black • needle and matching thread • toy stuffing or fabric batting*

**2** Stitch one wing to each body piece along the center back seam.

**4** Stuff firmly with toy stuffing or scraps of fabric batting. Slip stitch the gap securely. Sew a beak in position and glue on felt for the eyes.

# Tree Scratching Post

*The ultimate indoor gym equipment, this de luxe tree-style scratching post will spare your furniture all sorts of punishment.*

## You will need:

*cat scratcher • tape measure • green fabric • batting • lining • scissors • pins • needle and matching threads • staple gun*

*For further embellishment, why not add the robins to the tree too?*

**1** Measure all round one of the platforms on the cat scratcher and cut a rectangle of green material, batting and lining as long as this and measuring approximately 6in wide, adding seam allowances.

**3** Machine along the curved edge, then cut into the corners and snip the curves. Trim the seams.

**2** Cut out curved tree shapes on one of the long sides. Then pin the three layers together.

**4** Turn to the right side and press flat. Top stitch along the curved seam, ¼in in from the edge. Fold the seams over on the top edge and machine along the seam. Staple around the platform. Make a "tree" edge for each platform. You can always cover the top in material too.

# Games to Play

Anyone who knits will know how much fun a cat can derive from something as simple as a ball of wool. Other common household items can be used as the basis for all sorts of games. Here are a few.

*Feathers*

*Elastic*

*Corks*

*String*

*Pom poms*

*A ball of string or wool can provide hours of fun. Keep an eye on things just in case your cat gets into trouble – don't leave her unattended with the toy.*

# Cotton-reel Racing

You need an empty cotton reel and a relatively uncluttered room. Kneeling at one end of the room, attract your cat's attention and roll the reel rapidly across the carpet towards the opposite wall: it'll naturally tend to veer and swerve. She will race after the reel and pounce on it either before it hits the wall or after it bounces off. If you are feeling competitive, score a point for yourself if the reel hits the wall before she catches it, or a point for her if she snatches the reel triumphantly before it gets there. Your cat will end the game at the appropriate moment by getting bored and walking away; traditionally this is the time to add up the scores and announce the winner. Award the winner a red ribbon.

*The best playmate your cat can have (besides you, of course) is another cat, even if they do chew an ear off once in a while. If your cat is of normally stable and equitable temperament, make sure she comes into contact with other cats as regularly as possible.*

# Pawball

Mark a pair of goalposts on the wall – or, even better, build a goal from cardboard or use an empty cardboard box. Your cat goes in front of the goal, as keeper. Roll a small rubber ball – not too fast at first – towards her. Once you've both agreed the game of Pawball has properly started, which may take some time, every goal you score counts as a point in your favor; every time your opponent catches the ball before it goes into the goal is a point against you.

## Elastic Jumping

*Tie something weighty to the end of a length of elastic, or thread a wooden ball onto a piece of wire. Bounce the weight just in front of your cat's nose.*

*Do this fairly gently at first so that she can catch the "prey", then start to increase the speed and height above her. Once she is engaged and the game is properly under way, start for real.*

*Score by awarding her a point each time the weight is caught, and yourself a point for every bounce on the elastic before that happens; at the end of the session, divide your own number of points by ten.*

## Chasing Shadows

Arrange the lighting so that you can cast shadows on the wall using your hands: make butterflies, fish, swans, rabbits, mice and a hundred other shapes – if you feel really inspired, make shadow puppets of favorite shapes from pieces of cardboard and ends of string. Once your cat's attention has been attracted, you can spend half an evening quietly by yourselves while your companion leaps enthusiastically, trying to catch the enticing creatures.

*Cats are adept at yoga and were using it for relaxation and deep meditation millions of years before human beings ever thought of it. So rather than teaching your companion, you'll be better off watching her and copying the poses you see her perform.*

# Your Cat and the Stars

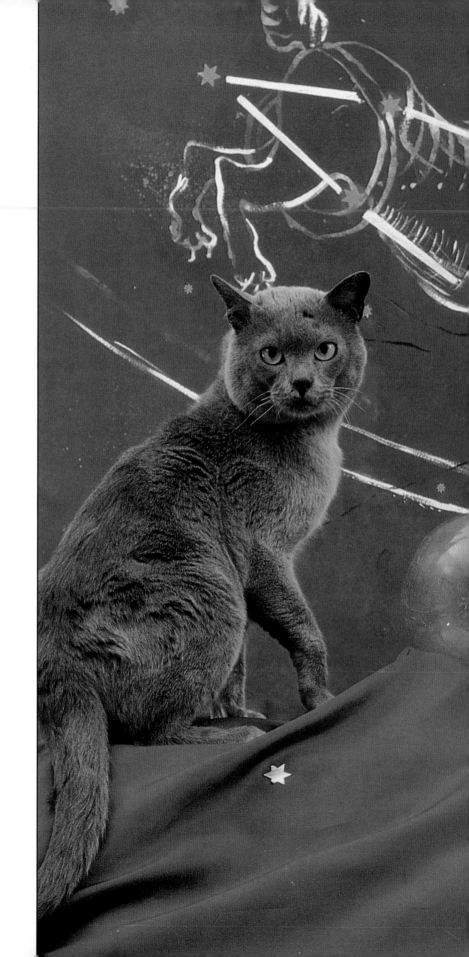

As your cat curls in the basket or langorously stretches out in front of the fire, the stars may seem a very long way away – but of course they directly influence her life as much as they do your own. Cat astrology has not yet become a refined science – there are still too many imponderables, especially the difficulty of ascertaining a cat's

precise time of birth – but you can make a start in understanding your companion's inscrutable character.

The observations in this chapter will enable you to fully please your pet – from selecting favorite foodstuffs and compatible colors, to understanding subtle mood swings and behavior more sensitively, however erratic and idiosyncratic they might appear to the untrained eye.

As human astrology is increasingly validated by overwhelming scientific and statistical supporting evidence, so cat astrology is only half a whisker behind. There is no doubt that cat characteristics are eerily predictable by star-sign – look up your companion's horoscope here and see for yourself!

Mystic Cat in characteristic pose, casting a horoscope.

# Aries

## 21 March–19 April

Aries cats are pushers: they are ever-ready to try something new as soon as it occurs to them. Unfortunately, they tend to have little staying power, so very often their ambitious plans come to nothing. They can be tremendous fun to be with, although you have to be prepared to be very tolerant – life with an Aries cat can be extremely rambunctious, so be prepared to say farewell to delicate ornaments and furnishings. Their independent streak can be a nuisance at times, but Aries cats compensate you for this with their unbounded affection.

*Aries cats are daring and outgoing and likely to be explorers*

*Give your Aries kitten its own house to destroy before it destroy yours*

*Red is the color and football is the game*

*If you don't have a trash can in the alley, give your Aries cat your leftovers instead.*

★ *Compatible cats*: Leo; Sagittarius
★ *Compatible owners*: same as cats
★ *Favorite color*: red
★ *Lucky number*: 9

★ *Favorite food*: fish of all types – particularly fish from trash cans
★ *Greatest dislike*: being kept for long periods in an enclosed space

★ *Other cat who may share this starsign*: Orlando the Marmalade Cat
★ *Attributes*: enthusiasm; independence; devotion; fecklessness

# Taurus

## 20 April–20 May

Taurus cats tend to be slow-moving and take a while making up their minds about something: once it's been made up, however, you may find it next to impossible to deter them. A Taurus cat will give you unswerving loyalty and friendship, but beware of one thing: Taurus cats are slow to anger, and this may give you the illusion that they never lose their tempers. But they do, and the eventual outburst can be very vigorous indeed. So be sensitive and considerate to your Taurus cat, and make sure you are consistently harmonious and concessionary.

*Sardines for supper*

*Give your Taurean cat a hideaway all of its own so that it always has somewhere that it can call home*

*Taurus cats will give you unswerving loyalty and friendship*

*Pastel-colored pussy boots for trips to town*

★ *Compatible cats*: Gemini, although be prepared for fights; Libra
★ *Compatible owners*: Taurus
★ *Favorite color*: pastel shades
★ *Lucky number*: 11

★ *Favorite food*: sardines
★ *Greatest dislike*: instability of any kind, such as frequent house moves – although fidelity to its owner enables it to cope

★ *Other cat who may share this starsign*: Dinah (from *Through the Looking-Glass*)
★ *Attributes*: loyalty; good-nature; temper

# Gemini

## 21 May–21 June

Gemini cats are usually frisky individuals, and among the most entertaining of all felines. Their frequent, unpredictable mood swings can be unsettling, but, once you are used to them, are a constant source of pleasure. Gemini cats are insatiably curious, and will pry into everything. Be sensitive to your Gemini cat's moods: just because she seems full of *joie de vivre*, don't assume she is unfailingly happy.

*Gemini cats are nosey so keep titbits and treats out of sight*

*Geminis are full of whims and fancies so it is impossible to predict what foods they will want. You may make a mistake!*

*Gemini cats have little patience and they are likely to throw their feet in the air at the slightest obstacle*

*Yellow and gold are a Gemini cat's favorite colors*

★ *Compatible cats*: Taurus
★ *Compatible owners*: Capricorn
★ *Favorite color*: yellow and gold
★ *Lucky number*: 3

★ *Favorite food*: Gemini cats are notorious for going off foods, so have several choices to hand
★ *Greatest dislike*: boredom

★ *Other cat who may share this starsign*: Thomas O'Mally
★ *Attributes*: curiosity; energy; bounciness; indecisiveness

# Cancer

## 22 June–22 July

Cancer cats tend to be sensitive creatures and devoted pets so long as you are as attuned to their moods as they are to yours. A Cancer cat will have a strongly developed sense of what is fair and what is not, so be prepared for some early "discussions" as you establish whose territory is whose. Cancer cats can be very good "watchcats": they become extremely territorial, and will see off other animals, including dogs much larger than themselves.

*Being sensitive souls, Cancer cats do not like to be upset*

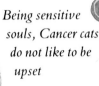

*Cancer cats can be very good "watchcats"*

*Even the smallest Cancer kitten will have a go at a dog if it is invading its space*

*Ring the changes for the daring Cancerian with a fruit cocktail*

★ *Compatible cats*: Scorpio
★ *Compatible owners*: Scorpio and Aquarius
★ *Favorite color*: earth tones

★ *Lucky number*: any number but 13
★ *Favorite food*: mixed, interesting food of different textures
★ *Greatest dislike*: emotional upset

★ *Other cat who may share this starsign*: Old Possum
★ *Attributes*: moral rectitude; sensitivity; possessiveness

# Leo

## 23 July–22 August

The lion is the king of cats, and most Leo cats assume themselves to be wild and regal. If you bring a Leo cat into your home, expect it to be in no doubt as to who is going to be in charge. Initially they can seem haughty and unapproachable, but once you have earned the friendship of a Leo cat, you will have a friend for life. Leos can be difficult with other cats who are not prepared to be pack-followers; they will regard it as their right that their food is served first and that their helping is significantly larger. So be prepared for some initial upsets if introducing a Leo cat to others.

*Leo cats often behave and even look like lions*

*Puppies have an annoying habit of being disrespectful, which rubs Leo cats up the wrong way*

*An imperial purple feather boa for an imperial cat*

*Leos like the very best things in life, such as fresh salmon*

★ *Compatible cats*: Aries, Leo
★ *Compatible owners*: Aries, Taurus or Leo – someone with a strong character

★ *Favorite color*: imperial purple
★ *Lucky number*: 1
★ *Favorite food*: salmon
★ *Greatest dislike*: puppies

★ *Other cat who may share this starsign*: Shere Khan (from *The Jungle Book*)
★ *Attributes*: entertaining; self-centered; theatrical; responsible

# Virgo

## 23 August–22 September

Virgo cats tend to be quiet, self-effacing, neat and exact, and may seem to be remarkably cool to your approaches. Don't be misled into thinking that this is a sign of arrogance – far from it, because Virgo cats, while often highly intelligent, tend habitually to underestimate their own worth and be consequently shy and unable to believe that you are so devoted to them.

*Full of confidence in her favorite green coat*

*Once Virgo cats are convinced you love them, they will return your adoration in full measure*

*Virgo cats hate any form of emotional insecurity so treat them with care and respect*

*Bland creamed cod fish jazzed up in a fishy mold*

★ *Compatible cats*: Capricorn
★ *Compatible owners*: any sign
★ *Favorite color*: green
★ *Lucky number*: 7, though 6 will do

★ *Favorite food*: a general inclination towards blandness might suggest creamed cod fish
★ *Greatest dislike*: not being loved

★ *Other cat who may share this starsign*: Cat Ballou
★ *Attributes*: sensitive; self-obsessed; reserved; smart

# Libra

## 23 September–23 October

Libra cats can be sociable and charming, and normally can be persuaded to see things your way. They generally take a long time to think things through but, as with Taurus cats, once they have come to a decision it can be next to impossible to divert them from it. They generally get on well with people and with other cats, and are usually prepared, after the necessary period of decision-making, to join in wholeheartedly with whatever the rest of the gang has determined to do. Once a Libra cat has decided to trust you, you must be worthy of that trust: any betrayal would be cruel.

*Libra cats do not like big dogs, possibly because their emotional equilibrium is upset.*

*Although pink is a Libran's favorite color, pale green and blue are also popular choices.*

*Libra cats dislike living alone, and need a happy and lasting relationship.*

*Mackerel for dinner.*

★ *Compatible cats*: Taurus, Aquarius
★ *Compatible owners*: no special preferences, although Libra cats do seem to get on particularly well with Sagittarians

★ *Favorite color*: pink
★ *Lucky number*: 19
★ *Favorite food*: mackerel, probably because of the scales
★ *Greatest dislike*: large dogs; ghosts

★ *Other cat who may share this starsign*: Top Cat
★ *Attributes*: arrogance; sociability; sulkiness; determination; indecisiveness; idealism

# Scorpio

## 24 October–21 November

Of all cats, Scorpios are likely to be the most promiscuous – in every sense of the word – they are the animals for whom the term "alley cat" could have been invented. They also tend to be the most psychologically complicated and interesting of all cats, although their natural egocentricity can be tiring at times. They give you the outward manifestations of affection easily enough – they will make up to anyone, if they think it is in their interests to do so – but earning their deeper love can require great patience on your part. Once you have done so, however, you could hope for no better companion.

*Watch out for the egocentricity of Scorpio cats – they like the limelight*

*Scorpio cats can be little devils*

*Make your Scorpio cat a maroon cushion for her to sit on during her moody moments*

*If you are on a tight budget but want to treat your Scorpio cat, settle for a plate of tomatoes*

★ *Other cats*: Cancer
★ *Owners*: another Scorpio can be the best bet – if you're a bit of an alley cat yourself, then this might be your ideal pet!

★ *Favorite color*: deep red or maroon
★ *Lucky number*: 111
★ *Favorite food*: caviare and tomatoes
★ *Greatest dislike*: being kept in at nights

★ *Other cat who may share this starsign*: Fritz the Cat
★ *Attributes*: sensitivity; spirituality; intense loyalty; temper and moodiness

# Sagittarius

## 22 November–21 December

Although their characters can sometimes be flawed by over-eagerness – they have a tendency to act first and think afterwards – Sagittarian cats can be the finest pets of all. They have a certain honesty that is unusual in felines, and they are generally prepared to demonstrate their affection for you in a boisterous, good-humored fashion. Sagittarius is quite a strong sign, so the Sagittarian cat usually gets on well with others and also, notably, with dogs.

*Purchase a double bowl so that you can give your Sagittarian cat a choice of foods at the same sitting*

*Sagittarian cats have a tendency to like dark colors mixed together, so plaids are an ideal fabric for them*

*Oddly enough, Sagittarian cats get on well with dogs*

*Sagittarians make enthusiastic and good-natured pets*

★ *Compatible cats*: Aries or Leo
★ *Compatible owners*: Aries or Leo
★ *Favorite color*: dark colors
★ *Lucky number*: 22

★ *Favorite food*: Sagittarian cats like a constantly varied diet
★ *Greatest dislike*: bureaucats and time wasters

★ *Other cat who may share this starsign*: Tom (of *Tom & Jerry*)
★ *Attributes*: enthusiasm; dynamism; good-nature; simplicity

# Capricorn
## 22 December–19 January

Like their human counterparts, Capricorn cats usually have the habit of confronting life's obstacles head-on, tending to charge through them rather than trying to devise ways of avoiding them. This can be both a strength and a weakness. Despite this gung-ho attitude, they often remain calm in difficult situations, and this has given them the reputation of being callous, calculating cats. Do not be deceived! A heart of gold lurks within.

*Capricorn cats love being groomed and being dolled up*

*If you give your cat chicken, make sure that you remove all the bones*

*Capricorn cats are often superficially reserved*

*Capricorn cats have a particular penchant for black chic*

★ *Compatible cats*: Virgo
★ *Compatible owners*: Sagittarius
★ *Favorite color*: black and brown
★ *Lucky number*: 12

★ *Favorite food*: fish and poultry, although very adaptable – often like vegetables more than most cats
★ *Greatest dislike*: locked fridges

★ *Other cat who may share this starsign*: Pussy Galore (from *Goldfinger*)
★ *Attributes*: intriguing; courageous; devoted; reliable

# Aquarius

## 20 January–18 February

Like Scorpio cats, Aquarian cats can be psychologically complex, but they lack the broody, dark aspect of the Scorpio cat; this may render them less interesting, but it also makes them a lot easier to live with. Gregarious by nature, they can nevertheless reject all their current companions once they are convinced they are unlikely to get their own way today. Many Aquarian cats have artistic aspirations; though they can be creative without following through on their ideas. Aquarian cats also have a highly spiritual element to their psychological make-up – they revel in the New Age.

*Allow your Aquarian cat to fully explore her mystical side by buying her a crystal ball*

*Lightly poached cod is a favorite*

*Aquarian cats love anything that is a deep shade of blue*

*Being creative and artistic, Aquarian cats are likely to be untidy*

★ *Compatible cats*: Libra, Pisces
★ *Compatible owners*: Capricorn, Pisces
★ *Favorite color*: electric blue

★ *Lucky number*: 8
★ *Favorite food*: poached cod
★ *Greatest dislike*: having to pay attention to detail

★ *Other cat who may share this starsign*: Irena Dubrovna (from *Cat People*)
★ *Attributes*: artistic; mystical; open; individualistic; unpredictable

# Pisces

## 19 February–20 March

Pisces cats are the hippies of the feline world. Friendly and sympathetic, often quite shy, they have good intentions but are generally too lacking in concentration to put them into practice. They tend to bumble along from day to day, never quite getting their act together but always somehow emerging from every difficulty unscathed. They are exceptionally affectionate – probably too much so for their own good.

*Piscean cats are ideal for fun and games*

*Any exotic fish will go down well – shark, swordfish or squid*

*Piscean cats tend to be very emotional*

*A fishy ornament for a fishy cat*

★ *Compatible cats*: Aquarius, Libra
★ *Compatible owners*: no preferences
★ *Favorite color*: sea-green
★ *Lucky number*: 2

★ *Favorite food*: any exotic fish – of course!
★ *Greatest dislike*: Pisces cats seem to have no particular detestations

★ *Other cat who may share this starsign*: The Cheshire Cat
★ *Attributes*: indecisive; genuine; good-spirited; reserved; vague

# Cat Perks

However much we love our companions, we have to acknowledge that their contemporary lifestyle is not entirely natural to them. Good owners are constantly aware of this, and always try to provide those little extras that make their deserving companions feel comfortable and special. Celebrations come infrequently during the year, so think of inventing a few new ones and have a regular routine of treats and pampering sessions as special gifts for deserving kitties. In this section you'll find suggestions and inspirations for hundreds of tiny touches that make all the difference.

For celebrations, special days and just for fun, pamper your pal with luxuries and the things she loves. If it's the thought that counts, there are inspirations here for a hundred sensitive gestures and sensational surprises.

Using very simple craft skills – all explained and shown in this chapter – you can make hundreds of treats and spectacular gifts for your companion, and personalize them in dozens of different ways.

# Gifts

Every day should be a special day in your cat's life, so there's no need to wait for Christmas or a birthday. Presents can be practical – a new bowl, for example – or joyously frivolous. The most important thing is that they are given and received with love . . .

*Whether sucked . . .*

*nibbled . . .*

*. . . or chewed, every gift from you will provide the kinds of spiritual sustenance, moral nourishment and physical pleasure that feed the inner cat.*

# Birthday Album

*A book to chart your cat's family tree, to hold photographs, and for noting down favorite recipes and important events and dates.*

## You will need:

*hardback notebook • patterned paper • pencil • scissors • PVA glue • construction paper • paper doilies • gold spray paint • craft knife • pictures of cats and flowers • ribbon*

**1** Place the book on the wrong side of the patterned paper. Draw a margin of about 1½in around it. Cut the paper to this size. Cut off the corners to create mitred joins, then glue the paper to the cover.

**2** Cut two pieces of construction paper to fit inside the front and back of the cover, leaving a small margin down the inside. Stick the paper in position. To decorate the cover, spray paper doilies with gold paint and cut them into pretty shapes. Also cut out flowers and pictures of cats from postcards, photographs and wrapping paper. Glue a ribbon onto the cover allowing enough at each end to tie a bow. Then add the decoration to the book.

*A purrrrsonal record of your cat's life.*

# Cat-o-Fish Tails

*Make a puppet out of cardboard for your cat, and the two of you can have hours of fascination watching it twitch and jerk. The basic design can be adapted to make rabbits, mice, fish or other cats.*

You will need:

*construction paper • soft pencil • craft knife • acrylic paints: purple, green, blue, red and black • paintbrush • ribbon • PVA glue • colored string*

**1** Draw all the pieces of the puppet onto construction paper – two legs, a torso, two arms, a cat's face and a collar. Cut out all of the shapes then paint all the pieces, detailing the design. Glue the head and collar onto the torso.

**2** When dry, glue a piece of ribbon onto the front of the torso to make a cummerbund. Glue another piece to the back of the face to make a hat.

**3** Pierce two holes at the top of each limb and four holes in the torso onto which each limb will be attached. Tie a knot in a piece of string and thread it through from the front of the torso through each arm and back through the other hole in the torso. Tie off in a knot at the front. Make sure the arms are loose enough to move up and down. Take another piece of string and repeat for the legs.

**4** Take a piece of string and tie it to make the connecting string between the arms and legs. Leave a length as the draw-string.

**5** Then cut a goldfish shape out of construction paper, paint it and tie it to the end of the middle string.

*Hang this magnif-i-cat mobile within your cat's reach and watch her go wild – as she pulls the tail the limbs fly up . . . be prepared to make another one shortly.*

# The Sacred Image

Your cat is central to your life, so celebrate her importance – and flatter her – by glorifying her image in tributes both serious and amusing. Needlecrafts, collage, painting, framing . . . the methods are many, and the results will provide beautiful objects and wonderful reminders of your companion through the stages of her life.

*Immortalize your cat by making a wall plaque of her portrait.*

*Capture those early days in a cross-stitch sampler.*

# Cross-stitch Sampler

*Samplers make distinctive adornments for any home, so embroider one specially to hang above the cat basket, to show how much you·care.*

**1** Draw your design onto graph paper using colored pencils or pens.

## You will need:

*graph paper 10 squares to 1in • colored pencils or pens • 11-count cross-stitch fabric in cream • embroidery hoop • basting thread in contrasting color • sewing needle • tapestry needle, size 26 • stranded cotton in a variety of colors*

**2** Place the fabric in an embroidery hoop. Mark the center of the canvas with colored thread, as shown.

**3** Work the sampler in cross stitch using the method shown on page 95. Remember that the top diagonal stitches of each cross should always slant in the same direction.

# Pop-art Portrait

*The ultimate gift for contemporary cats, an Andy Warhol-inspired portrait of your special pet.*

You will need:

*photograph of your cat • liquid typing erase • four sheets of different colored paper • scissors • pencil • glue • red acrylic paint • tissue or paintbrush • four sheets of colored paper approximately 12 × 9½in • white cardboard*

**1** Choose a favorite photograph of your cat, ideally one which has good contrast, and whiten out the area around the face. Make some bold white marks to delineate ears and eyebrows.

*Sexier than Marilyn and more irresistible than a can of soup, your cat makes the perfect model for a $4.5m-style portrait that costs only pennies to reinterpret.*

**2** Photocopy the image onto colored paper, enlarging it to cover an area 6 × 6in. Make four copies, all on different colored pieces of paper. Cut out the faces.

**3** Trace outlines of parts of the faces onto the leftover scraps of paper and cut out. Stick the colored highlights onto faces of a contrasting color.

**4** Dab paint lightly onto a couple of the faces with a tissue or a paintbrush.

**5** Glue the four cat faces onto the four sheets of colored paper. Mount these onto the white cardboard.

# Christmas Cat

Roast turkey with stuffing, presents around the tree, a stocking full of surprises . . . there's a lot to interest your cat around Christmas time. A festive meal with all the trimmings, designed exclusively around your cat's favorite foods, is just the start. Think of making a special cracker or two out of rice paper, with savory treats inside. Or make an Advent calendar, with special titbits behind each "window". Or go to town and fill a stocking full of delectable treats. All in all, there are hundreds of ways you can make Christmas a memorable time not just for your cat but also for yourself.

*Christmas card cats in the perfect feline tableaux.*

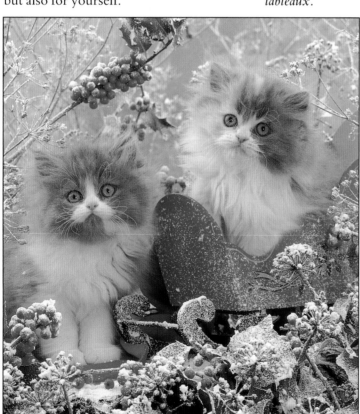

# Queen of the Nile Gift Wrap

*Bastet was the Egyptian goddess who appeared as a cat. All cats were sacred to her, so what could be better as a gift-wrap design?*

**1** Trace the templates of the cat and symbols on page 93, and draw them onto thin cardboard. Cut them out.

**3** Use a gold-leaf effect to highlight certain areas. Place the stencil over a painted area. Dab through the card with glue and place a layer of gold leaf over the glue. When dry, remove the stencil and gently brush and blow away any excess leaf.

## You will need:

*tracing paper • soft pencil • thin cardboard • craft knife • sheet of textured plain paper • masking tape • stencil brush • acrylic paints: black, terracotta and purple • PVA glue • gold leaf*

**2** Place the stencil onto the sheet of paper and secure it with masking tape. Using the stencil brush, apply the paint but do not overload the brush with paint. Move the stencil to another part of the paper until you have covered the whole surface.

*This cat-festooned paper will provide as much fun to play with as the present inside.*

## Stocking Fillers

*A tasty
sisal fish*

*An elastic
pom pom*

*A furry
mouse*

*A spider
on elastic*

## Christmas Cookies

*Treat your kitty to a real
Christmas feast of these
festive fishy cookies.*

*8oz plain wholewheat flour
1 × 7oz can pressed
cods roe
2oz vegetable fat
1 egg*

*The perfect
Christmas TV
snack.*

**1** Preheat the oven to
350°F. Put all the
ingredients into a mixing
bowl.

**2** Mix into a soft dough,
adding a little water if
the mixture is too stiff.

**3** Turn out onto a floured
surface and roll out to
about ¼in thick

**4** Cut out the cookies and
place on a baking sheet
and cook in the oven until
crisp and golden. Allow to
cool and then store in an
airtight tin.

# How to Communi-cat

You've taken every necessary measure to ensure your companion's physical well-being, what about the inner cat? Good diet, plenty of exercise, comfortable surroundings, warmth and affection – plus a little work on your own manners – will normally ensure that you have a happy, well-adjusted, secure and fulfilled cat, but you can go further towards ensuring her emotional well-being by learning how to communicate. Here are some tips.

*Cats have a million ways of talking among themselves, but need encouragement to communicate with you.*

## Speaking

Cats rarely use sounds to communicate with each other – except when threatening to fight – whereas we use them all the time. Domesticated cats have noticed this and learned to employ distinctive calls when wanting to be fed or let out, when welcoming you home or even triumphantly bringing in a new item of prey from the garden to "share" with you. At these times your cat is making a big effort to talk to you, so learn the meanings of these different calls and respond appropriately.

## Trusting

Kneel down in front of your cat and, with your hands behind your back or well out of the way, slowly lean forward until your face is just an inch or two from hers, keeping your eyes open. Because you are presenting your vulnerable eyes so close to her you are showing that you're neither aggressive nor frightened – in short, that you're a trusting friend. If she feels like responding in kind, you'll find your nose being gently brushed by her nose or forehead. (Do not under any circumstances try this with a cat whom you do not know well, or with a neurotic, unpredictable cat.)

## Eye Contact

Catch her attention and lock eyes. Then, without making a big production of it, blink very slowly, just once, and keep your eyes locked on hers. If she is relaxed and content, the reply will come in the form of a responsive slow blink. It may take a while before she catches on that you're making the effort to communicate in "cat language" (which this is), but gradually you will be able to say "I love you and you love me" whenever you want to.

*All cats are wary and defensive at first. But trust, and showing you are not afraid to be vulnerable, breaks down aggression and protective display, and eventually results in a gentle response.*

## Telling the Tale

Different cats can use different tail signals, so study your own cat's individual movements. In general, however:

- *tail held in a low curve*: confident and content
- *tail held upright*: alert, confident, possibly aggressive
- *tail upright and waving*: possibly angry, more likely just keenly interested
- *tail wrapped around snoozing cat, or gently beating the floor with a slow, regular thud*: completely relaxed and secure
- *tail between the legs*: insecurity, possibly fear
- *tail wrapped around the legs*: fear

*This tail curved around the legs shows nervousness . . . while the upright wave indicates keen interest.*

*Held upright, the tail says, "I'm confident, and maybe even a little full of myself today".*

## Ready to play?

A cat who's busy relaxing may want to keep on snoozing, but if you want a cuddle, approach gently and stroke very lightly, just brushing the tips of the fur. If in the mood for affection, your cat will raise her head and respond with a lick of your hand or face, or may move her head up towards your hand, indicating that some more vigorous stroking would be very much appreciated. In the latter case, if the cat stretches out both forelegs to the front, this will be a signal that she is prepared to foresake her nap for more animated play.

*If your cat responds to an advance by leaning into your strokes or fondling and nuzzling back, she is graciously indicating that more touching would be acceptable!*

# The Magnificat Day

Days like Christmas will of course be times when you want to pay your cat particular attention, but obviously you won't be able to concentrate your entire focus on your cat – you will have human obligations to fulfil as well. So, every now and then, allocate a day completely to her, designating it a Magnificat Day.

All the activities that your companion loves best can be packed into this single day. Presents, gourmet meals, friends to visit, snoozing, playing outside, and a few games as well. For the day, you could endeavor to communicate in "cat" rather than in "human" as much as possible, and set a quiet time aside for a long period of stroking and grooming.

*Play soft and mellow melodies to enhance your companion's catnaps.*

*The complete playtime toy for a kitten . . . it also keeps your furniture from being destroyed . . . a present for both of you.*

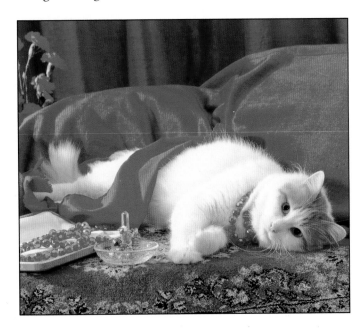

*The purrrrfect pampered pussy cat.*

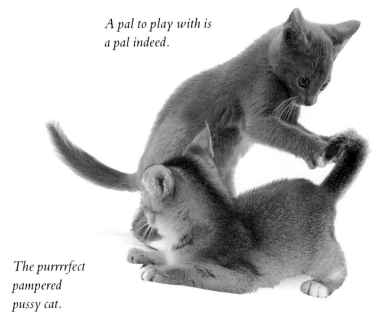

*A pal to play with is a pal indeed.*

*Stroking is an integral part of the Magnificat Day. Except when your companion wants to snooze, eat or hunt in the garden, make sure you offer a lot of affectionate stroking and tickling – show her she's the most important person in your world!*

# Cod in Parsley Sauce

*The purrrrfect ending to a purrrrfect day.*

*3oz cod fillet, skinned*
*1/3 cup/3 fl oz milk*
*1 tsp butter*
*1 tsp flour*
*1 tsp chopped parsley*

Poach the cod in milk until cooked. Remove and allow to cool. Using a whisk, beat the flour and butter into cooking liquid and slowly bring to a boil, stirring until thickened. Add parsley and allow to cool. Pour the sauce onto a plate and add the fish.

*A possible end for the Magnificat Day: settling down in front of a roaring log fire for snoozing, stroking, and just being together.*

# Templates

You can either use the templates the same size as they are reproduced here or enlarge them. To use the same size, simply trace them, transfer onto paper and cut them out. To enlarge, either use a grid system or a photocopier. For the grid method, trace the template and draw a grid of evenly-spaced squares over your tracing. To scale up, draw a larger grid onto another piece of paper. Copy the outline onto the second grid by taking each square individually and drawing the relevant part of the outline in the larger square. Finally, draw over the lines to make sure they are continuous.

## Stenciling

Stencils can be cut from thin cardboard or special stencil cardboard. Trace the pattern onto the cardboard then cut it out with a craft knife. Secure the stencil firmly to the surface to be painted. To achieve a good, clean shape, the paint needs to be thick so that it does not run and you should use the paint sparingly. Apply the paint using a light dabbing motion. Wait until the paint has dried before moving the stencil and painting the next shape.

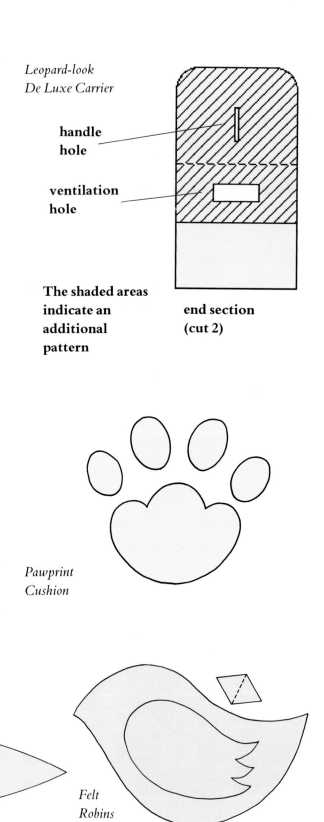

*Leopard-look De Luxe Carrier*

handle hole

ventilation hole

**The shaded areas indicate an additional pattern**

end section (cut 2)

*Pawprint Cushion*

*Felt Robins*

*Plaid Kitty Coat*

*Queen of the Nile Gift Wrap*

*Goldfish-bowl Ball*

# Basic Sewing Techniques

*Basting*

## Basting

This is a temporary stitch used to hold seams together before sewing. The stitches should be between ¼in and ⅜in long.

*Applying Bias Binding*

## Applying Bias Binding

Pin the bias binding on the right side of the fabric with right sides facing

and raw edges aligning. Baste and machine stitch in position along the raw edges with a ¼in seam allowance. Remove the basting stitches, turn the free edge of the binding over to the wrong side of the fabric and turn it under itself to create a clean edge. Slip stitch with matching thread to secure in place.

*Machine Appliqué*

## Machine Appliqué

Machine appliqué is quick and hardwearing. Cut out the motif, then pin and baste in position on the main fabric. Set the sewing machine to a close zig zag or satin stitch and sew around the edges of the shape so that the raw edges are covered completely.

## Quilting

To achieve good results, the layers of fabric you are working with – usually top fabric, batting and backing – need to be secured together before you begin to stitch. This will prevent

the layers from slipping out of position. To do this, lay the backing fabric wrong side up on a flat, hard surface. Lay the other two layers over the top, ending with the top fabric, right side up. Pin, then baste the layers together. For small pieces you can use safety pins instead.

You can then either machine- or hand-sew the quilt. For quilting by hand, work the design using small, evenly spaced running stitches. If quilting by machine, work a small practice piece. A "walking foot" fitted to your machine will help prevent the fabric layers moving and causing puckering.

*Tailor's Marks*

## Tailor's Marks

This is the most accurate way to transfer markings from a paper pattern onto double fabric. With the pattern still pinned in place, make a tiny slit through the paper across the symbol to be marked. Using a double thread, baste several loops through both layers. Remove the pattern, gently ease the fabric apart, and cut the loops.

# Basic Stitches

## Running Stitch

Running stitch is one of the most commonly used stitches. It should be used for hand-quilting designs and gathering, keeping the stitches small and evenly spaced on both the front and back of the piece. Work running stitch by passing the needle regularly in and out of the fabric to create the pattern.

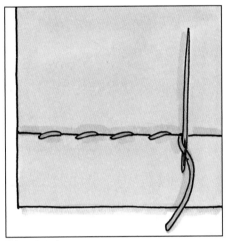

*Slip Stitch*

## Slip Stitch

Slip stitch is used to join together two folded edges. When joining two folds, the stitches are almost invisible and are worked from the right side of the fabric. Pick up a couple of threads of the single fabric and carefully slip the needle through the fold for about ¼in. Draw the thread through to make a tiny stitch.

*Satin Stitch*

## Satin Stitch

Satin stitch looks easy but some practice is needed to work it neatly. It is used for filling in and outlining. Ensure the fabric is always held tautly in a frame to prevent puckering. Carry the thread across the area to be filled, then return it back underneath the fabric as near as possible to the point from which the needle emerged.

*Stab Stitch*

## Stab Stitch

Stab stitch is used for attaching things to fabric almost invisibly or for quilting through many layers and it is literally a stabbing movement. Bring the needle up through the layers of fabric, then make a tiny stitch and push the needle through underneath. Make a larger stitch under the fabric and repeat.

*Cross Stitch*

## Cross Stitch

Cross stitch is the best known of all embroidery stitches; it was used by the ancient Egyptians and more recently for the samplers made by nineteenth-century schoolchildren. It is worked in two parts, and the top stitches should always lie in the same direction. For large areas, work a row of diagonal stitches from right to left, then complete the crosses with a second row of diagonal stitches in the opposite direction.

# Index

Accessories, 24, 28
Aromatherapy, 52, 53
Astrology, 66–79

Bathing, 46, 47
Beauty treatments, 44–55
Beds, 8–11
Birthday album, 82
Bow tie, 29
Brush, fancy, 50

Carriers
  jungle, 12
  leopard-look, 13
Captain Kitt's Cabin, 11
Cat-o-fish tails, 83
Celebrity fishcakes, 40
Cheese please, 33
Chicken
  cheeseburger, 36
  sardine crust, with, 37
Christmas cat, 86
Coat, plaid kitty, 22
Cod in parsley sauce, 91
Collars, 20, 21, 25
  catmaiden, 26
  jewelled, 27

Communication, 88, 89
Cookies, Christmas, 87
Cotton-reel racing, 64
Cuisine, 30–43
Cushion, pawprint, 15

Decorations, 18

Easter cuisine, 40
Eggstacy, 32
Elastic jumping, 65
Entertaining, 38

Fish
  celebrity fishcakes, 40
  cod in parsley sauce, 91
  crispy trout pieces, 34
  fabulous fishballs, 39
  kedgeree, 35
  kipper supreme, 35
  mackerel magic, 35
  nutrition, 34
  reflections, 19
  roe dip, 41
  salmon mousse, 39
  sardine soup, 32
Fruit cocktail, 38

Furniture, feline, 16

Games, 64, 65
Gift wrap, 86
Gifts, 82
Goldfish-bowl ball, 61
Grooming, 48, 49

Halloween, 41

Kedgeree, 35
Kipper supreme, 35

Leads, 25

Mackerel magic, 35
Massage, 54, 55
Mice and cheese plates, 42
Mouseburger bites, 33

Nutrition, 34

Organ duet, 37

Paper mice, 60
Pawball, 64
Pawprint cushion, 15
Perks, 80–91

Place mat, 43
Pop-art portrait, 85
Privacy screen, 17

Rabbit chasseur, 37
Robins, felt, 62
Roe dip, 41
Rugged pursuits, 62

Salmon mousse, 39
Sampler, 84
Sardine soup, 32
Sewing, 94, 95
Shadows, chasing, 65
Snoozing, 58, 59
Soft furnishings, 14
Sports and games, 56–65
Stocking fillers, 87

Toys and games, 60–65
Tree scratching post, 63
Trout, crispy pieces, 34
Turkey, 41
TV snacks, 32

Valentine's day, 40
Vanity case, 51

# Acknowledgements

The publishers would like to thank the following for creating items for photography: Thomasina Smith for the Jungle Carrier, Leopard-look Carrier, Skyscraper Privacy Screen, Fish Reflections, Mice and Cheese Plates, Birthday Album, Cat-o-Fish Tails, Pop-art Portrait and Queen of the Nile Gift Wrap; Lucinda Ganderton for the Pawprint Cushion, Fancy Brush and Vanity Case; Paul Jackson for the Paper Mice; Carole Hart for the Plaid Kitty Coat, Catmaiden Collar and Jeweled Collar; Wendy Massey for the Bow Tie, Goldfish-bowl Ball, Felt Robins and Tree Scratching Post; Petra Boase for the Pussy Place Mat and Lesley Grant for the Cross-stitch Sampler.

The publishers would like to thank Sue Hall, Melinda Ellis and Hazel Taylor for their help during the photography sessions and Georges of Chelsea, 6 Cale Street, London SW3 (0171 581 5114) for their generosity in loaning items for photography: screen p.16, ornaments p.18, green coat p.22, t-shirt, black coat and harness p.25, and additional grooming equipment and toys.

They would also like to thank Philip Yeast Products Ltd, Park Royal Road, London NW10 7JX (0181 965 7533) for the wendy house p.10; Canac Pet Products, Becks Mill, Westbury Leigh, Westbury, Wilts (01373 864775) for the tartan mat p.14; Something Special Ltd, Baden House, The Square, Marazion, Cornwall TR17 0AP (01736 710206) for the draught excluder p.16; Cover up Designs Ltd, 9 Kingsclere Park, Kingsclere, Nr. Newbury, Berks RG15 8SW (01635 297981) for cat bowls and food jars; Purves and Purves, 83 Tottenham Court Road, London (0171 580 8223) for cat plates; Cosmo Place Studio, 11 Cosmo Place, London WC1 (0171 278 3374) for hand-painted china plates; Companions, 12 South Grove, Tunbridge Wells, Kent TN1 1UR (01892 529648) for the plaque p.84 and Emap Pursuit Publishing Ltd for the transparency of the four-poster bed p.10.